BRONTË
COUNTRY

Upper Ponden and the heights of Oakworth Moor seen from Delph Hill near the Alcomden Stones –
a vast sweep of the Brontë Moors.

BRONTË
COUNTRY
Lives & Landscapes

PEGGY HEWITT

Foreword by Juliet Barker

with Photographs by Simon Warner

SUTTON PUBLISHING

First published in 1985 under the title *These Lonely Mountains*
by Springfield Books Ltd

This revised edition
first published in 2004 by
Sutton Publishing Limited · Phoenix Mill
Thrupp · Stroud · Gloucestershire · GL5 2BU

British Library Cataloguing in Publication Data
A catalogue record for this book is available from the British Library

ISBN 0-7509-3823-4

Typeset in 10.5/13pt Galliard.
Typesetting and origination by
Sutton Publishing Limited.
Printed and bound in England by
J.H. Haynes & Co. Ltd, Sparkford.

Contents

	Foreword by Juliet Barker	vii
	Acknowledgements	ix
	Introduction	x
1.	Uproar in Haworth	1
2.	Martha, the Professor and t'Free Schooil	7
3.	Glory and Grief on the Brontë Moors	12
4.	Lily Cove – Tragic Balloonist and Liberated Lady	19
5.	Way of the Worth	24
6.	Lament for the Brontë Bus	31
7.	A Windmill at Newsholme	37
8.	Coppin'-on at Ponden	41
9.	Facts of Life and Death	46
10.	Of Moles and Men	51
11.	Old Timmy – Weaver and Legend	54
	(or When Tilda Returned Timmy's Love Piece)	
12.	Quarries and Violins	59
13.	Rahnd an' Rahnd with Arthur	64
14.	Portrait of Patrick	69
15.	Wycoller	74
16.	Incumbents and Trustees	81
17.	Nature's Gentleman	86
18.	Stanbury and the School under the Sky	91
19.	The Many Sides of Sir Isaac	100
20.	Steam Up in the Worth Valley	105
21.	Cool, Calm and Collected	112
22.	Ponden People	117
23.	Methodism in his Madness	123
24.	The Company of Ghosts	127

'Wuthering Heights' – the old farmhouse of Top Withens, 1977.

I'll walk where my own nature would be leading:
It vexes me to choose another guide:
Where the gray flocks in ferny glens are feeding;
Where the wild wind blows on the mountain side.

What have these lonely mountains worth revealing?
More glory and more grief than I can tell:
The earth that wakes one human heart to feeling
Can centre both the worlds of Heaven and Hell.

Emily Brontë

Foreword

When Charlotte Brontë wrote an introduction to her sister Emily's novel, *Wuthering Heights*, she felt obliged to apologise to the readers. 'The wild moors of the north of England can have for them no interest;' she wrote, 'the language, the manners, the very dwellings and household customs of the scattered inhabitants of those districts, must be to such readers in a great measure unintelligible, and – where intelligible – repulsive.'

I feel no need to make such an apology in introducing this book. The Brontë moors, as we now call the South Pennines, are known and loved throughout the world, precisely because the Brontës have made them famous. The bleak and beautiful wilderness of the moorland round Haworth was a source of daily inspiration to the Brontë sisters in their lives, in their novels and in their poetry. Without them, we would have had no *Wuthering Heights*, no *Jane Eyre* and no *Tenant of Wildfell Hall*; nor would we have the 'peculiar music – wild, melancholy, and elevating' of Emily's sublime poetry. The moors are the key to understanding the Brontës, yet the sense of permanence and immutability which they create is an illusion. This unique haven for wildlife and precious place of solitude in a heavily industrialised West Riding is under constant threat of development, from roads and reservoirs to telegraph poles and wind turbines.

The people who live here are changing too, as the traditional hill-farming, which sustained the area for hundreds of years, disappears under the weight of economic pressure and bureaucratic red tape. Even as late as the 1980s, when this book first appeared, it was still possible to meet people from Haworth and the surrounding villages who might have walked straight out of the pages of *Wuthering Heights*. That is why *Brontë Country* is such a valuable book. It is a celebration of a way of life which has, by and large, vanished like the early morning mists on the moors. Unlike them, that way of life will not return.

It would be wrong to create the impression that this book is some sort of melancholic funeral oration. Peggy Hewitt's lively and affectionate description of 'the language, the manners, the very dwellings and household customs of the scattered inhabitants of those districts' is full of humour, wit, eccentricity and colour. As such, it is a fitting tribute to the people of this inspirational corner of Yorkshire.

Juliet Barker

Vince Whitaker, lately of Rush Isles Farm, Ponden, provided a necessary service as carter of goods in the Stanbury area.

Acknowledgements

My first thanks must be to the Worth Valley itself; for the down-to-earth kindly people I knew in my childhood, for the feeling of homeliness I remember and where I learned to enjoy the freedom of fields and streams and moors.

To appreciate the 'today' of a place it is essential to know about its past, and I am grateful to Ian Dewhirst, former Reference Librarian at Keighley Library, for making available to me archives and works of reference, and also to Juliet Barker for the engrossing hours I spent in the Brontë Parsonage Library when she was Librarian and Curator there. One of my happiest memories while writing this book (and every little boy's dream) is riding on the footplate of a steam train between Haworth and Oxenhope one cold and frosty winter morning (not to mention sitting by the warm fire in the waiting room at Oxenhope Station afterwards) – and for this I am grateful for the co-operation of the dedicated folk of the Keighley & Worth Valley Railway.

I have been privileged to share the memories and the knowledge of many people who became friends in and around the Worth Valley; without them this book would not have been written . . . particularly Keith Houlker, formerly of Wycoller, Keith Spencer of Ponden, Peter Snaith of Haworth, and also the late Martha Heaton whom I remember with great fondness. There are many others who sadly are no longer with us but their stories are captured within these pages and their voices come freshly to us today.

Last but by no means least my thanks go to Simon Warner for the pleasure of working with him, and to my husband Tom for his continual patience and support and for his lovely vignette drawings which enhance the book.

Peggy Hewitt
Spring 2004

For Maurice Colbeck, former Editor of Yorkshire Life *magazine, in gratitude for his guidance and patient encouragement of my early literary efforts.*

Introduction

Emily Brontë was right in her poem to describe the Brontë moors as 'mountains' even though they are a mere 1,500 feet in height at Wuthering Heights and Crow Hill. John Wesley, a frequent visitor to Haworth with his brother Charles, also referred to them as mountains in his Journals and James Mitchell, the 'Old Gentleman' mentioned later in this book, writes in his *Dendrologia*, 'And now, Moses-like, after forty years wandering, I have retired . . . to the Mountains in the West of Yorkshire to enjoy the reward of temperance and industry'. The Brontë moors obviously had the same effect on these three very disparate people. Hard and unyielding in some respects they might be, yet they have all the grandeur and mystical qualities of much loftier places, and when you have come to terms with their nature you have discovered a little bit more about yourself.

In any weather the moors are beautiful. When the mist swirls in the valleys the crests of the hills sail like ships on a silent sea; then it creeps up to engulf even these and the outlines of old farms are like fading monotone photographs of long ago. And through the mist, in soft echoes, drift the hopes, the passions and the fears of the folk who have lived and worked and died there. Many of these farms have long been empty, their floors are deep in the dung of the moorland sheep that shelter there through the worst of the weather. In some, discoloured wallpaper, once carefully chosen, hangs in pathetic ribbons from the walls like wisps of hair clinging to a skull. The stone hearths are cold and bare, where children sat and wriggled their toes out of clogs to warm them at the blaze, and the wind eddies the mist as it creeps through sockets of empty doors and windows. Slowly these farms sag into the landscape, some disappear altogether, but at last there is a gleam of hope. Yorkshire Water, which owns most of them and the land around, for many years refused to re-tenant them because of 'possible sewerage seepage' to the reservoirs. We tried to buy an old and decaying and lovely farmhouse above Sladen Reservoir about thirty years ago but without success. Now, comparatively recently, this farm building has been sold and renovated as a private residence. Life has returned to it and it will stand firm through the changing seasons as it has done for hundreds of years.

Summer is a passing thing, gone like a dream, abdicating in royal robes of heather to golden autumn and the turning bracken. The moors spread beneath an infinite blue sky and by the streams the little valleys are generous with blackberries and the orange fruit of rowan and wild rose. Purple shadows invade the gullies in the evening and the plaintive cry of the curlew hangs in the still air.

*Winter on the Brontë
moors.*

When winter grips the moors the snow lies deep, piled against the walls and filling
the ravines, and narrow sheep tracks stand out like veins on the white hillsides.
Waterfalls and springs are captured with icicles, the bogs give a firm footing, and
wisps of snow lie in the crevices even until April.

Then suddenly the starlings gather and clamour down by the reservoir and the
fields are full of cheeky black-faced lambs with wide dark ears. The valleys are white
again, this time with May blossom, the song of the skylark 'lifts earth to heaven' and
the sweet smell of frost-freed heather roots hangs in the air. The wind is fresh,
blowing from the west, born in a gully by Penistone Crag; that same wind that
plucked at the cloaks of genius over a hundred and fifty years ago. Seagulls hover and
glide along the valley, bound for the high moors above Wuthering Heights, and the
dreams and the spirit of a gifted girl are there, riding on their wings, and her laughter

mingles with the music of running water as they hover over Wuthering Heights, tumbling her and her dreams to earth.

'I was only going to say that heaven did not seem to be my home; and I broke my heart with weeping to come back to earth, and the angels were so angry that they flung me out into the middle of the heath on the top of Wuthering Heights, where I woke sobbing for joy.' Emily speaks to us from the pages of *Wuthering Heights*.

On the Brontë moors past and present, fact and fiction, are curiously mingled, interdependent, and it is almost impossible to separate them. Many years ago, while I was thinking about writing this book, I was walking over the moors one late spring evening towards Stanbury. The setting sun picked out every dip in the landscape and the unfurling bracken fronds were an iridescent green. The drystone walls and forgotten farms stood stark among the sheep-cropped turf and a skylark hovered and sang just about where the sky merged from steely blue to pearl. 'Wuthering Heights' was a dark blur below the horizon, and above it hung a sliver of new moon, trailing the evening star in its wake. A gentle wind breathed through the translucent tufts of cotton grass, and moths fluttered softly among the young heather and harebells . . . an evening that inspired Emily Brontë as she wrote the last paragraph of her novel.

Gradually I overtook a stout little figure, in sensible brogues, with a book clutched in one hand. *Wuthering Heights*, of course. I slowed down to walk with her and we chatted. Then . . . 'It's wonderful to think', she said, 'that Heathcliff walked along this very path.' I looked once again at the flickering moths and breathed in the smell of peat released by the cooling earth. The shadows were creeping out of the gullys now and stealing across the moors, and the moon was bright in a deepening sky. 'Oh, but you're wrong,' I thought. 'Heathcliff is even now walking along this path, searching, and Cathy is hiding from him in that small hollow over there.'

Several years ago an unusual visitor came to Haworth. She was Mary Dunjeva, a Russian Jew, and she was an actress and a poet. While she was living in a kibbutz in Israel she had read *Wuthering Heights* and since then her dream had been to give a short presentation of it in Haworth. So she came, and gave her presentation, and we walked on the moors. 'In Russia', she said, 'you have open spaces with isolation – on Haworth moors you have solitude.'

Charlotte Brontë would have agreed with her, although she herself was not completely at one with the moors. To achieve that, she wrote, one must be a 'solitude-loving raven – no gentle dove . . . because from the hill-lover's self comes half its charm'. And yet, in a loving tribute to Emily after her death, Charlotte binds the spirit of Emily forever with the moors.

'My sister Emily loved the moors. Flowers brighter than the rose bloomed in the blackest of the heath for her; out of a sullen hollow in a livid hillside her mind could make an Eden. She found in the bleak solitude many and dear delights, and not the least and best loved was – liberty.'

Peggy Hewitt, Spring 2004

1

Uproar in Haworth

Visitors in their thousands, from all over the world, push themselves through the too-narrow north door of Haworth Church, firmly believing that they are entering the building where the Brontë sisters worshipped and where their father, the Revd Patrick Brontë, was curate for forty-one years.

In fact, the Brontë Church was demolished in 1879 at the instigation of the Rector, the Revd John Wade, and great was the public uproar – although most of the protest seemed to come from outside the village – and even the national newspapers took up the story. The people of Haworth themselves were curiously unmoved by the whole affair, appearing if anything to support Mr Wade's proposal, but they could have been swayed by the fact that Mr Michael Merrall, an influential millowner and employer in Haworth, was prepared to donate £5,000 towards a new

Haworth Old Church as the Brontës knew it. It was demolished in 1879. On the left is the house of John Brown, the Sexton and friend of Branwell Brontë. On the far left is the school built by Patrick Brontë. Notice the absence of trees in the churchyard.

building. Many also regarded the Merralls as being synonymous with Haworth Church – they were generous both with their money and their time, and the position of churchwarden seemed to be a Merrall monopoly.

A 'very lively' public meeting was held to discuss Wade's proposition on 28 May 1879, and among those opposing it were the Lord of the Manor, Mr W.B. Ferrand, Mr Isaac Holden from across the valley in Oakworth, and Mr T.T. Empsall, representing the Bradford Historical Society. On the other hand, Mr G.S. Taylor of Stanbury, whose family claimed to have connections with Haworth Church for 'longer than any other family in the township', backed Wade, as did the local schoolmaster who described Haworth Church as 'perhaps one of the most ugly and hideous buildings in the country'. He could just have been right. With its light-restricting gallery and high box pews, its enormous pillars and three-decker pulpit inconveniently situated half-way along a side wall, the *Daily Telegraph* (joining in the row) said of it, 'There is not much beauty in Haworth Church that it should be desired.' Nevertheless, that paper did suggest that it should be left standing as a Brontë memorial and that a new one be built elsewhere.

The church as it existed then had stood only for a century and a quarter, although there had been several buildings on the same site. There is evidence of a 'field kirk' there as early as 1317, but none of them had the colourful history of the building it was proposed to demolish. It was from here that William Grimshaw thundered forth his word of God to packed congregations, and the church saw stirring times during the Methodist Revival when men such as John Wesley and George Whitefield preached to thousands who thronged the churchyard to hear them. And then, of course, there were the Brontës.

By this time Haworth had been described as a 'shrine' to that family, no doubt causing pangs of irritation to ruffle the clerical calm of Mr Wade, Brontë's successor, and Wade's critics had accused him of trying to stamp out the Brontë image and of perpetrating an 'act of vandalism'. It is true that the Brontë pew had already been removed from the church some years previously for no apparent reason, and this latest proposition was described in a leading article in the *Standard* as an 'outrage upon public feeling'. What probably added fuel to Brontë fire was the fact that although Patrick had laboured long and faithfully in Haworth and had repeatedly requested that it should become a separate parish from Bradford, this had not been granted in his lifetime, and poor Patrick remained 'Curate' to the end of his days. The separation of the parishes did in fact take place in 1864, three years after Patrick's death, and in 1867 the Revd John Wade was given the status of Rector, thus becoming the first Haworth incumbent to hold that title.

Wade defended his proposition to pull down the church by saying that it was unhealthy and did, in fact, smell, and documents which came to light again comparatively recently after being lost for many years would seem to substantiate this. They include plans of the old church which show the actual positioning of many old graves and two vaults, and the grim fact is that some of these graves were actually underneath the stone floor. One of the vaults is that of the Brontës, the other remains a mystery.

The Revd John Wade, successor to Patrick Brontë. He was the first Rector of Haworth and instigated the pulling down of the Brontë Church.

The argument swayed backwards and forwards but at last Wade had his way and on 14 September 1879, 'before a stone was removed', the final services were conducted in the Brontë Church, and thousands attended to pay their last respects to the historic building.

It was demolished at great speed, except for the tower; this forms the greater part of the present tower in the south-west corner of the building and is the only bit of the Brontë Church to remain. The old box pews, inscribed with the names of Haworth families who have lived there for generations, were removed – 'most of the oak of which they were constructed being carried away as relics or made into articles to serve as ornaments on sideboards'. The occupants of the offending graves were also removed and more hygienic resting-places found for them, but the Brontë vault, containing all the members of the Brontë family except Anne, who is buried in Scarborough churchyard, remained untouched. It is to the right of the chancel steps in the present building, marked by a bronze plaque on the floor, and when the heather blooms on the moors there is usually a sprig placed close by.

On Christmas Day 1879 Mr Michael Merrall laid the corner-stone of the new building, using a silver trowel presented to him by Mr Wade, and in a cavity below it was placed a phial containing a history of Haworth Church, written on parchment, and some coins and a newspaper of the time.

For over a year church services were held in the old Sunday School where Charlotte Brontë had taught, and where she carefully examined the needlework and knitting of the day pupils, until on 22 February 1881, on a typically cold and snowy day, the new church was consecrated by Bishop Ryan of Bournemouth, deputising for the Bishop of Ripon who was indisposed. (There was no diocese of Bradford at that time and Bradford parish was under the authority of the Bishop of Ripon.)

The new church was built slightly to the north of where the old building had stood, possibly because of the close proximity of graves in the churchyard, and this could account for the cramped position of the north door and also for the fact that the tower is now at the end of the south aisle instead of the nave.

The church was built of local stone, and gifts for it poured in, probably one of the most beautiful being the alabaster reredos which stands behind the Lord's Table. It depicts Leonardo's *Last Supper* and was given by Mrs Wade. The pulpit, a single decker this time, is also in alabaster, beautifully carved with tracery panels, the central one portraying *The Walk to Emmaus*, and was the gift of Mr George Firth of Bradford. A fine alabaster font with marble columns was given by Mrs George Merrall. Beautiful stained-glass windows and an oak table were donated by people for whom Haworth Church was a special place, and many smaller gifts were sent from people with Haworth connections. There was also the initially promised gift of £5,000 from Mr Michael Merrall and a surprise contribution of £700 which had been collected, unsolicited, by the not-very-affluent parishioners. The total cost of the whole work was estimated to be £7,000. Unfortunately, Michael Merrall lived only a few months after the new church was consecrated, but the Merrall family continued to play a big part in the life of the church in its new building.

Strangely enough, considering the loud protests by Brontë enthusiasts at the pulling down of the old church, it took eighty-five years for a fitting memorial to be raised to the Brontë family in the new church, in addition to the simple plaque

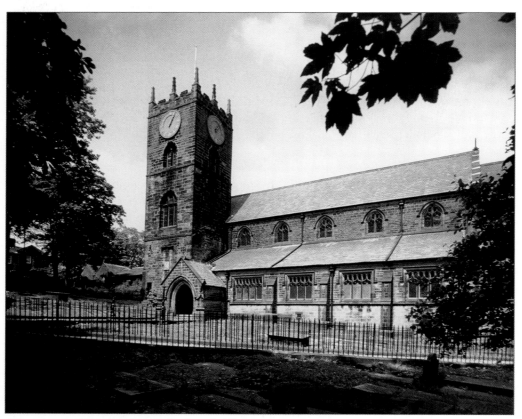

The present Church of St Michael and All Angels, Haworth, consecrated in February 1881. The lower two-thirds of the tower are all that remains of the Brontë Church. On the left the Brontë Parsonage Museum can just be seen.

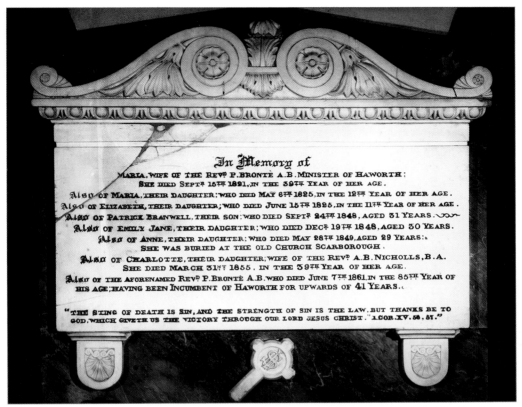

The Brontë memorial plaque, now in the Brontë Chapel in Haworth Church.

which was transferred to the new building. There had been rumours that Arthur Bell Nicholls, Charlotte's widower, had plans to erect a memorial to his late wife, but nothing came of it. He had stayed with Patrick Brontë as assistant curate until the old man died and had hoped that the living of Haworth would be offered to him. When it was not, he was bitterly disappointed and came out of the ministry, returning to Ireland where he took up farming and eventually married his cousin.

It was not until 4 July 1964 that the Brontë Chapel, gift of Sir Tresham Lever, was dedicated by the Bishop of Bradford (by this time Bradford had become a diocese) and some of the furnishings from the old church came home. These included Grimshaw's seventeenth-century Communion Table (before which Charlotte and Arthur Bell Nicholls made their marriage vows – it is a poignant reminder of their short-lived happiness), and also his inscribed candelabra, and the original Brontë plaque adorns one wall. The chapel was constructed entirely by local craftsmen, many of whom were church members.

In 1928 the new Rectory on West Lane was blessed by the first Bishop of Bradford, Bishop Perowne, and the old Parsonage was bought by the industrialist Sir James Roberts, local boy made good, and presented to the Brontë Society. It

The building in the centre, at the top of Haworth Main Street, was formerly the Yorkshire Penny Bank, and the Brontë Society used the upstairs rooms as offices and museum. In 1928 Sir James Roberts bought the old Brontë Parsonage and presented it to the Brontë Society, which moved from its rather cramped quarters at the bank to its present worthy position.

became a busy museum, a place of pilgrimage – the Brontës were in possession of their old home, if not their old church.

But a family such as this cannot be confined by stones and mortar – their spirit lives on in the very air that is Haworth, and on the open moors that nourished their genius and inspired them to write the books and poems that are world-famous.

2

Martha, the Professor and t'Free Schooil

The little Japanese gentleman bowed low over the bowl of yellow chrysanthemums he was holding and the early autumn breeze, fresh from the Brontë moors, gently ruffled the petals of the flowers. 'These are for you – you are so kind to me, a stranger,' he said, as Martha Heaton opened the door of her cottage in answer to his knock.

Yoshimasa Kiyohara, Professor of English at Kobe University, was visiting Leeds University in September 1977 principally to study the writings of the Brontë sisters. The English he could cope with, but the Yorkshire dialect in *Wuthering Heights*, as spoken by Joseph, the Earnshaws' retainer, was too much for him, and on a visit to Haworth he had gone to the Tourist Information Centre for help. They had pointed him to Martha Heaton, expert on the local dialect, a visit had been arranged, and he duly presented himself, unofficially accompanied on his walk from Haworth by a Brontë dog.

Martha and Yoshimasa got their heads together over *Wuthering Heights* until a word in the professor's copy had even Martha stumped. So confident was she in her knowledge that she decided it must be a misprint – and sure enough, reference to another copy proved her right.

'Maister, coom hither! Miss Cathy's riven th'back off "Th'Helmet uh Salvation" un' Heathcliff's pawsed his fit intuh t'first part uh "T'Brooad Way to Destruction". It's fair flaysome ut yah let 'em goa on this gait.' You can see Yoshimasa's dilemma. There had to be a playful demonstration of the word 'pawsed' (kicked) before he could understand what it meant, and Martha also had to explain how to make porridge Haworth-style so that Yoshimasa could follow some of Joseph's actions.

'He came on a Tuesday – we were having stew so he had some with us,' and this visit proved to be the beginning of a long friendship between the two of them. Yoshimasa returned to Japan after his English studies and compiled a simple guide book in Japanese of the Brontë country; he visited Martha several times and they corresponded regularly.

Baking day for Martha Heaton at Hawksbridge.

Martha, who lived at Hawksbridge, was a moorland legend, a member of the illustrious Heaton family who first came to the area in the fourteenth century. One branch of the family built Ponden Hall and later became friends of the Brontës, and Martha was an expert on both family and local history. It helped that she inherited the prodigious Heaton memory and also their love of books, but she was sad that she missed their lovely auburn hair.

One of her earliest recollections was a visit to Uncle Dobson at the age of two. 'Father took us from Westfield Farm to Hebden Bridge in a pony and trap and then we got on a train for Accrington. A lady gave me a jelly sweet on the train – I shall never forget that jelly sweet.' Sweets must have been a rare treat for Martha. Uncle Dobson had been an engine driver, but one day he was going to fill an oil can when a 'silent engine' ran into him. He lost both legs as a result but got no compensation – except one free train journey a year. Yet when he came to stay with them it was always a red-letter day.

Martha started Oxenhope School at the age of four, although she could read before that, and was under the tuition of a Miss Asenath Hill. 'I wore a cloth dress woven at the local mill, a frilly white needlework pinny – we were only allowed two pinnies a week – black hand-knitted stockings held up with black elastic and a large woollen shawl draped over my head and fastened with a big pin. It was a good day when shawls went out of fashion and shoulder capes came in – all the girls had long hair and lice tended to breed in the shawls. The boys wore knee-length corduroy trousers and Norfolk jackets; sometimes they were made of fustian which had a funny smell. Their white celluloid collars were wiped over with a soapy cloth every morning and of course we all wore clogs. We took dinner in a tin box and a lady at a nearby house made tea for us to drink.' Martha was at school during the Boer War and clearly remembered needlework lessons when she sewed handkerchiefs with pictures of Lord Roberts and other generals printed on them.

Almost all the scholars attended Sunday School; Martha herself went to Hawksbridge Chapel and her first Sunday School prize, presented when she was three, was literally 'worn away with much use'. She remembered being in trouble at home for 'wasting' five shillings on a book of Tennyson poems – 'It was a lot of money in those days' – and, at the slightest encouragement, could reel off poetry, especially Brontë poetry, by the hour. Martha was a popular speaker at local meetings and even wrote plays which she produced herself at local chapels and churches.

Just above Martha's cottage is Leeshaw Reservoir, and Martha was taken as a child to watch this being built. The sight of the water swallowing up the valley evidently made a great impression on her, and many years later she wrote a novel about the place as it was before the reservoir came – *Sunhill*. When Yoshimasa saw Martha's typed *Sunhill*, he offered to take it back to Japan and have it duplicated for her. Unfortunately, when it was returned 'all the folds were the wrong way round, Japanese-style, and it wasn't much good'. One of Martha's short stories, 'The Wild Rose Briar' (based on a poem by Emily Brontë), was enthusiastically taken to Japan and translated into Japanese by Yoshimasa – he thought it would be 'marvellous for his pupils'. Martha also wrote a short history of Hawksbridge Chapel, where she was a Sunday School Superintendent for sixty-eight years, and her own autobiography, *A Tale that is Told*. This begins: 'On Friday morning, 21st August, 1896, at 4.30 I was brought into the world by Mrs Mary Baldwin, the local midwife, who lived at Marsh, Oxenhope. I was given the name of Martha in memory of mother's sister, Martha, who had died in childbirth in June of that year.' A straightforward statement of life and death and continuance of 'family' on the Brontë Pennines.

Martha managed to do all this in spite of the fact that her education was basic – her mother, a busy farmer's wife, considered the education of daughters to be a waste of time, and at the age of twelve Martha went to work half-time at Banks Mill, Oxenhope, locally known as 'Brooks' Meeting' because it was sited near to where two streams converged. The third of nine children, she found even homework difficult to fit in because there was always plenty of housework to be done, and she never learned to play a musical instrument. 'I was more keen on reading, and loved walking.'

There was plenty of that, with the local 'walking days' the highlight of the year. Whit Sunday was Anniversary Day at Hawksbridge Baptist Chapel, and also at West Lane Baptist Chapel in Haworth, the two being under the same minister. On that day a long procession would form at Hawksbridge, Superintendents first, then women, girls, boys and men, decorous and in that order. Along the quiet country roads they went towards Haworth, until finally they were met by a similar procession coming the other way from West Lane. After the 'right hand of fellowship' had been exchanged, the two processions wended back to West Lane for a service that was always crowded to the doors and beyond. The following day, Whit Monday, these processions formed and united again to walk round the houses of local gentry to sing hymns. Each child carried its own mug and tea was dispensed at the appropriate time, together with 'walk cakes', rich with currants and peel and sticky with sugar, clothes baskets full of them, and sometimes even an orange as well. 'We were always told to take the oranges home with us, so that the peel didn't litter the gardens.' All up and down the valley, churches and chapels were 'walking' on Whit Monday, and those that could afford it hired a band. In retrospect at least, those days seemed to be full of sweet contentment, but Martha had one regret. 'I just missed a "Scott Scholarship".'

It was in 1638 that Christopher Scott left a building and annuities of £18 for the founding of a Grammar School at Marsh, near Haworth, and for the maintenance of a schoolmaster who was 'able and willing to teach his scholars Greek and Latin in such a commendable manner that they might be fit for either of the universities of Oxford or Cambridge'. The master himself was to be a graduate from one of these universities – Haworth had aspirations, even in those days.

Thus Haworth Free Grammar School, or 't'Free Schooil' as it was locally known, came into being. Trustees were appointed from the 'chief men of the township of Haworth', and eventually lands were acquired by the Trust. The school was permitted to take up to six boarders and was enlarged in 1818, with a house being built for the master. The Trustees were responsible for the school and the lands and found themselves dining their tenants twice-yearly on rent-days (or refunding 4*s* 6*d* in lieu!).

Some of the masters at 't'Free Schooil' were clergymen and 'Mr Donne' in Charlotte Brontë's *Shirley* was based on the Revd J.B. Grant who taught there. Another link with Charlotte – after his long and difficult courtship of her, Arthur Bell Nicholls stayed there just before they were married, and often the couple would walk across Church Fields together, between Marsh and Haworth, his tall figure stooping over the diminutive Charlotte in her long cloak.

With an annual salary of £30 in 1793, rising to £45 in 1842, the high standards stipulated by Christopher Scott regarding the master were not always easy to keep, and there was a corresponding drop in academic achievement by the pupils. In 1853 the Trustees were obliged to appoint a 'non-graduate', a William Summerscales of Keighley, described as a 'machinist', but in 1864 things looked like taking a turn for the better when the Revd Wm Patchett MA arrived on the scene, determined to reintroduce the classical nature of the school – and also to charge a fee of five to ten shillings per pupil per quarter. The horrified Trustees insisted that the school remain 'free', apart from the nominal sixpence per quarter for 'fire and stationery' already paid by the pupils. And this at a time when even National School children, mostly from poorer families, were having to pay tuppence or threepence a week for their education. Patchett did not achieve his goal; by this time things were at too low an ebb with only fifteen pupils attending, their Latin was sketchy to say the least, and in 1886 the Trustees reluctantly agreed to close the school. By this time the railway had improved communications with Keighley and new schools had been built both there and in the surrounding villages.

The Trust money, now invested in stocks, was used to set up six scholarships to the Grammar Schools in Keighley (it was one of these scholarships that Martha Heaton narrowly missed). With the Education Act of 1944 these in turn became unnecessary, and now each year the Haworth Exhibition Endowment Trust (Scott Exhibition) inserts an advertisement in the local paper inviting 'students whose parents reside (or if deceased were resident) in the ancient township of Haworth, which includes Oxenhope and Stanbury' to apply for a grant to aid their further education.

These grants come by courtesy of Christopher Scott, who died three hundred and fifty years ago, strong in his belief that children benefited from a knowledge of Latin and Greek. Nowadays they are more likely to lean towards Spanish or Russian, but he would be gratified to know that a few of his beneficiaries have entered Oxford, and thus his wishes when he originally set up the Trust are still being fulfilled.

The old school, now a private residence, Marshlands, is still referred to by some local people as 't'Free Schooil', and across the way, not far from the cottage where Martha Heaton lived with her sister Alice, stands Free School Farm, reminders of the time when Haworth had its own Grammar School.

3

Glory and Grief on the Brontë Moors

The Brontë moors present an air of permanence, as though they have been there for ever, which is almost right if you consider that their gritstone bedrock was formed two or three hundred million years ago. Until recently, by that time-scale at least, the moors were covered with forests, but by the twelfth century this protection of trees had disappeared from the summits, one reason being that originally the soil there was lighter and better for cultivation. Centuries of wind and rain have washed away this topsoil, leaving the moors of heather, bracken and bog as we know them, with the millstone grit either very close to the surface or completely exposed. At the same time settlements in the valleys grew bigger, trees were cut down as some became first villages and then towns – the huge forests had disappeared, and so had much of the richness from the soil.

The Brontë moors, therefore, would seem an unlikely place to farm, but nevertheless farming has gone on there for centuries. Many of the farms you see today have stood there for at least three hundred years, and there was often another building on the same site before that. These very old farms were known as 'long houses', and were simply one long single-storey building, which served as a barn at one end and family living and sleeping quarters at the other – sometimes a row of stones or a drainage channel separated the two ends. Eventually things became more refined, and although the buildings were still the same shape, a wall separated family from animals. A fireplace was built into this wall, with a stone 'speer' or screen as protection from draughts, and a door led through into the barn.

Initially the only outside door often led straight into the barn end, and as this was where the threshing also took place the word 'threshold' came into being. A unit of measurement for these farm buildings was a 'bay', a rectangle twelve by sixteen feet, this being the area necessary to accommodate a team of oxen.

The living quarters acquired an upstairs, at first just a half-loft with a ladder, and this was used for storage until rooms began to be built off the main building, usually for dairies or storage space.

Life was very basic for the hill farmers up to the beginning of the twentieth century, each farm being about 10 acres, self-contained and self-supporting. One thing the moors had in abundance was water, and each farm stood by a spring. Oats were grown on land that had to be rescued from the bracken as 'intake', the staple diet being porridge, with oatcakes or havercakes, which were hung over a rack or 'breead flak' and looked for all the world like speckled wash-leathers. Cows, sheep and pigs were kept for home use and a fat animal, slaughtered, salted or smoked, provided meat during the long winter months. In some old buildings, stone slabs used for the slaughtering of animals can still be seen, carved with runnels and holes, and if a spring ran beneath the house, the slabs were sited above it so that blood and offal could be washed away. Pigeon lofts were often built into barns, their occupants – together with hares, rabbits and sometimes chickens – being the only fresh meat available in winter. There is a district near Haworth locally known as 'Harehills', and this used to be riddled with the homes of these little animals. Poaching was not unknown, and home-made shuttles have been found for making nets for this purpose.

To augment the poor living wrested from the moors, every farm clattered to the noise of the handloom, and often the finished wool or cotton had to be carried for miles on foot to be sold at the Piece Hall at Halifax. Enterprising entrepreneurs occasionally acted as 'middlemen' and carters, making the profit of the weavers even less.

The old stone farms can be read like a book – deep holes in a wall indicate that tenterhooks were fixed there for stretching the cloth, groups of shallower holes round a stone doorpost were 'wuzzling holes', where stout sticks were pressed on which creels of wool were swirled to dry them after the scouring process. Sometimes a stone 'lant' trough can be found against an outside wall where urine was collected for the scouring, the ammonia content breaking down grease and lanolin in the wool, and often a stone channel ran through the wall from inside straight into the trough; those houses without channel or trough simply used a bucket. One characteristic of the moorland barn is the two large doors built in opposing walls – at threshing time they were both flung open to allow the wind to blow through and carry away the husks.

The people of the moors were superstitious, possibly because of the close proximity of the Pendle witch country. Single shoes and bottles of potions have been found in cavities, thought to have been put there to ward off evil spirits. Witch balls of coloured glass were hung in the windows in the hope that a passing witch, looking in and seeing her distorted reflection, would be frightened away. Unusually formed witch stones were hung from inside beams, and a long glass twisted rod, full of minute coloured beads, was sometimes fastened up in the hope that it would attract the attention of any witch who did get inside and distract her from her evil purpose. On the corner of the outside roof a stone 'kneeler' often protruded horizontally, no doubt a necessary piece of architecture, but this has been referred to as a witch stone – a place where a witch might rest and not trouble to come inside.

At one time it was usual for the family themselves just to occupy one heated room for living and sleeping, the upstairs having become a weaving chamber, and even quite recently, in comparatively comfortable times, some old moorland farmers retired for the night 'up to t'chamber'.

Times change, customs change, and in some slight respect the moors have changed, too. Many farmhouses are now just empty husks, sad relics of the families who have lived there, and who have tasted something of the glory and the grief of the Brontë moors; others have disappeared altogether, victims of a combination of harsh conditions and the local Water Authority, who have bought most of the farms and are loath to re-tenant them once they become empty because of possible sewage seepage to their reservoirs. Bracken encroaches on the hard-won patches of green that once surrounded the farms, and rushes grow where drainage ditches have become clogged and ineffective. Originally farmers were responsible for the paths that led to their farms, but when a farm disappears, who looks after the path?

Each year thousands of hikers in regulation gear of garish anoraks, woolly hats and heavy boots grind along the footpaths, with the result that they are deteriorating at an alarming rate. A few years ago the Countryside Commission stepped in to put matters right, with a little help from Bradford Metropolitan Council and the Job Creation Scheme, and something of a hornets' nest was stirred up in the process.

How does one preserve nature itself? Today parts of Haworth moors resemble nothing so much as a Diddyman's playground. Some of the local people are not amused, and Emily Brontë must be spinning in her vault. Neat little dykes, bridges and walls grace some of the footpaths, although a dressing of bright yellow sandstone chippings has already washed away, steps have been made at the steep

Once a farm and a home . . . now just a husk. Near Ponden.

An old stone gatepost on the way to 'Wuthering Heights'. No gate, no track, no farm.

parts to help the walker, and arrows, direction 'blobs' and notices have sprung up. A convenient little patio has been created at Wuthering Heights itself for picnickers, and log benches provided for them to sit on – it seems that people are no longer able to sit on the ground – and the old farmhouse itself, neatly squared off for safety, bears a close likeness to a barracks. Another reason for this, apparently, is to preserve it, but some people might argue in that case that it would be better to let it fall down altogether. A favourite walk from Ponden Hall to Ponden Kirk, where a little path wandered along the side of the valley above Ponden Clough Beck, has been spoilt because the path has been turned into a 'highway' for waterworks vehicles and rubble scattered to all sides.

The farms that still live are nearly all confined to the valleys now; one good thing that has happened is a scheme to plant more trees round them – 'shelter-belt' planting – and that must be a welcome development.

If one is not careful, the sense of liberation, of walking in a place out of time, usually engendered by the Brontë moors, could give way to a familiar feeling of being carried along on a modern conveyor-belt system. But this will not last. The reasons for all these 'improvements' may be admirable – the footpaths were becoming worn deep into the peat and have now been built up with stones, ashes (and the yellow chippings), and as they were in a bad condition walkers were making detours, thus creating areas of potential bog. But sooner or later nature will take over and the moors will regain their identity. Basically they are still the same, only mildly irritated, like a sleeping giant when a fly walks across his nose.

Haymaking at Stanbury.

But for the farmers still left in the Upper Worth Valley life has to change; no longer can they be self-contained, self-supporting, and with the land very much as it has always been, with the stone always there just below the surface, they must become competitive.

George Bancroft farmed in the valley for sixty years and knew its limitations. 'When it's ploughed time after time, it gradually moves down t'hill till you're down to nowt at t'top,' was his summing-up. During the war each farmer had to plough and sow a certain acreage, regardless, and a farmer across the valley accordingly did just that. 'They'd gotten it reet grand.' Then during the night came a thunderstorm and 'washed all t'top soil down to t'bottom in a heap – it were a reet mess'. Obviously, crops of any kind are no longer a good proposition for the Upper Worth Valley.

George looked back to his early days in the valley with fondness. Life was much harder then, but there was more fellowship and everybody knew everyone else. 'Fifty year sin' we were all struggling on together – not thinking about going to t'world's end to find something better.'

Seven to twelve acres are no longer a viable proposition for a farmer, so land has to be bought or rented either from a reluctant Water Authority or from 'off-comed 'uns' who simply live in the farms and commute to business in towns. 'It's ruining t'farming.' George himself had land dotted over a wide area. Indeed, for a long time his sheep grazed at Wuthering Heights and once, while taking a small flock up there, he lost them. 'Good God, wheer can they have gotten to?' Then he saw the kitchen door of Lower Heights Farm was open – the sheep had gone inside. Being ever one to take the bull by the horns, as it were, he marched in, round the large kitchen table, driving the sheep before him, and out of the door with a bright 'Morning' to the speechless farmer's wife.

Wuthering Heights (or Top Withens) has been empty since 1926, its last occupant being Ernest Roddy. Ernest was gassed in the First World War and after being advised to live in the country (he already came from Haworth), he set up as a poultry farmer there. When he finally had to leave, he returned to Haworth and assumed his old job of french polisher, plus postman, plus hawker of yeast. Every Tuesday he tramped miles round the farms with his yeast, which he sold for 1*d* an ounce but 'when he landed home at neet he wouldn't be worth the robbing,' was George's comment.

George and Hannah Bancroft outside their farm near Ponden. Winter is definitely winter on Haworth moors!

Although pigs are no longer kept on the farms, George remembered a rogue boar that turned nasty and killed another boar with its tusks. 'We got it roped up over a beam – I doan't know what would've happened if t'rope had broke – then we took a hammer and chisel and knocked t'tusks off b't'root.'

Sheep are the main stock now, wandering seemingly free over the moors until by a miracle they are rounded up for shearing or lambing. One wily farmer got wind that his neighbour was selling a flock of sheep at Clitheroe Market and went and bought them, putting them on his grazing adjacent to his neighbour's. He knew the sheep were 'hefted' to their old haunts and would soon move back there to feed – which they did.

Keith Spencer was a comparative newcomer to farming in the Worth Valley when I first met him but wouldn't have gone back to his painting and decorating business for worlds. He had extended his farm from 15 to 83 acres, 'as much as a man can look after himself without staff', and as well as pedigree French Charolais cattle and Suffolk cross sheep he also kept rare Japanese green peafowl, common Indian blue peafowl – and a pet fox whom nobody had told about BO. His interests ranged from architecture to local history, from photography and wildlife to antiques – an unusual farmer and a contented man.

George Nixon lived in Oldfield and his life was cattle orientated – by day he worked for the Milk Marketing Board and in his spare time he experimented, rearing bulls on intensive feeding. The bulls he kept inside, of course, and he cleaned them out but once a year – their shed was a place where fools might rush in but angels certainly would not. Once two bulls were 'bothering' just as George went into their shed and in a trice they had him head first in a trough full of cow cake. 'Anyway,' he said philosophically, 'you don't need to dehorn them, they're away before they get too dangerous.' Under intensive feeding, bulls are ready for slaughtering at ten months compared with the usual eighteen months. George bemoaned the red tape and expensive machinery which he felt was killing off the small farmer. 'We're even told how to dehorn our cattle. In the old days we simply cut a groove, put a rubber ring round it and it dropped off cleanly in three weeks. Now they have to be sawn off, and they ooze with matter.'

George remembered: 'Twenty years ago every small farm produced milk and the churns were collected daily from stands at the top of each drive, but a "golden handshake" from the Milk Marketing Board enticed the small farmer away from milk production – it wasn't economical for the tankers to collect it.' EU quotas have further inhibited milk production, and in Oxenhope tankers collect only a fraction of what was supplied in churns not all that long ago.

At Dixon Hill Farm, Jack Atkins leaned against his drystone wall and contemplated the valley where he had lived all his life, but for four years in the army. 'In the 1930s farming in the valley was bad,' so he went to work at Hattersley's Mill in Oakworth where the money was good – he earned 17s 0d a week and got 1d in the shilling spending money. After the Second World War he came back to full-time farming and, like George Nixon, groaned about red tape. 'If the Government tells you what to do they've probably got it wrong. During the war we were told to grow oats – nobody knew how any more and it was a flop. In the old days they developed a corn that would ripen even in these hills – it even grew at Wuthering Heights.'

Jack and his son Richard were into calf rearing and sheep, and found it difficult to compete with the big farms. 'The contour of the land makes things hard and here we're 900 feet above sea level.' Jack felt that farming in the area had gone full circle, with machinery so expensive that it was necessary to sell three-quarters of the stock to pay for it, he would probably have been better off if he'd milked ten cows by hand. About the future of farming, 'I don't know which way it will go.'

It seems that modern times have laid a question mark over Emily's 'lonely mountains' and the farmers are coping in their different ways – the glory and the grief are still there but the question is – which is going to get the final upper hand?

4

Lily Cove – Tragic Balloonist and Liberated Lady

The year was 1906 and the village of Haworth was *en fête* for its eighth Annual Gala. Previous galas had turned out to be half-hearted, interest seemed to be on the wane, and some blamed the steep ascent of Main Street, saying it was just too much for the procession after its long walk from Crossroads. But this year the Committee had expectations that the gala would be a success. They had arranged a special event that they hoped would draw the crowds – Miss Lily Cove, the young aeronaut, was billed to make a balloon ascent from the Gala Field on West Lane and descend by parachute further up the Worth Valley near Ponden. Little did they know that ripples from their special attraction would reach as far as the Palace of Westminster.

Lily Cove had arrived in Haworth the day before the gala with her employer, Captain Frederick Bidmead, and they had taken rooms at the old White Lion Hotel at the top of Main Street. She had charmed everyone with her outgoing, easy manner and soon made friends with the young daughters of the proprietor. To them she must have appeared a glamorous, exotic creature, one of the new 'liberated' women, definitely interesting and slightly shocking. Some of the older folk disapproved of the way she was known to show off her legs in tights for her balloon ascents (she was described in the press as a 'good-looking, well-proportioned young woman') and no self-respecting lady cavorted about the countryside with a gentleman who was not her husband, even if he was her employer!

Lily, who had lived in the East End of London with her widowed father, a journeyman shoemaker, had been employed by Captain Bidmead in his balloon manufacturing business, but soon he began training her as an aeronaut, with the two of them jumping together in double harness. She had already made twenty solo ascents, the last one at Cambridge, and she was barely twenty-one years of age.

On the day of the gala about six thousand people turned up on a hot and airless afternoon, Saturday 9 June. Excitement was high in the Gala Field as the breathless procession finally arrived – comic cyclists, austere members of Haworth local council and the Keighley Board of Guardians, squads of ambulance men, and horses – light, draught and heavy – with their harnesses gleaming in the sunshine. Methodist

Sunday Schools had provided four tableaux – 'Britannia and her Colonies', 'Different Nationalities', 'Indian Hoop Drill' and 'The Last Scene in Cinderella', and there was judging to be done and speeches to be made before the main attraction could take place. Mrs R.E. Weatherhead of Bingley spoke on behalf of the Victorian Nurses Fund, beneficiaries of the gala, saying 'During the month of May, no less than 282 visits had been made by nurses. That meant an average of 70 visits per week, into the homes of many who would otherwise not receive proper attention.' Haworth and Kildwick Brass Bands stood by, ready to blast off the minute the speeches ended, in loud competition with the Keighley Wiffan Waffen Wuffen and the Haworth Bingem Bangem Comic Bands – there was Bailey Brothers Punch and Judy, ventriloquial and conjuring displays by a Monsieur Ducarel, and exhibitions by local Athletic and Ladies' Physical Culture Clubs. But all eyes kept wandering to the gas balloon, and to the young woman who stood waiting by it – Miss Lily Cove.

At last the speeches were ended – the moment everybody had been waiting for had arrived. Lily perched herself on the precarious seat under the balloon and Captain Bidmead checked the leather harness she wore round her waist and over her shoulders. Her parachute was attached to the harness by hooks at the shoulders, and was also fastened to the balloon mesh by a cord calculated to snap when she jumped. Then things began to go wrong. The inflated balloon would not rise, and after six attempts the ascent was abandoned – but only for that day. Loath to disappoint the crowd completely, Lily, looking rather pale, announced that she would make another attempt on the Monday evening. Captain Bidmead declared that it was the first time in his experience that this had happened, and finally put it down to the fact that the gas in the balloon was too impure and heavy for the atmosphere of that airless afternoon.

The following day Lily and Captain Bidmead occupied themselves with mending a tear that had appeared in the balloon during their attempt of the previous afternoon, then went out to tea in Haworth at the home of Albert Best, Secretary of the Gala Committee. The unsuccessful balloon attempt had unnerved Albert and he tried to persuade Lily to call off the ascent planned for the following day, but she would have

Lily Cove, tragic balloon parachutist. Maybe she had listened at suffragette meetings in Victoria Park in the East End of London where she lived and was seeking her own personal freedom. We shall never know.

Captain Frederick Bidmead, Lily Cove's employer. An experienced aeronaut himself, he had appeared at the Keighley Gala in June 1898, standing in for Auguste Gaudron, who was appearing at the Alexandra Palace that day. Unfortunately the cords of the parachute became entangled with the mesh covering the balloon and refused to snap when he jumped. He dangled below his balloon, helpless, terrified to move in case the balloon uptipped. Somewhere in the clouds, he lost his cap, which was later retrieved from the local sewerage plant, and also one of his medals along the way.
The balloon drifted some 27 miles 'as the crow flies', and finally came down in the grounds of Stapleton Hall, near Pontefract, where he received much-needed succour.
The following day he returned to Keighley – by train – scratched but with his usual aplomb, and received a hero's welcome.

none of it. She was a lass of spirit and quite determined. She was also an impetuous girl. During tea the Salvation Army came to sing outside the house of Albert Best in the course of their Sabbath rounds of Haworth and Lily dashed out to join them, singing heartily to their tambourine accompaniment.

The following evening the crowds turned out again to watch Lily's balloon ascent from the Gala Field, and prominent among them was Charlie Merrall, the local mill-owner's son. He was apparently infatuated with the brave young aeronaut. At about twenty minutes to eight on that June evening the balloon was once again released, and this time rose without incident, passing over the cheering, cap-waving crowds with Lily fluttering a handkerchief in salute from her trapeze-like seat.

Away towards the moors it floated like some huge dandelion clock silhouetted against the evening sky – away towards Ponden until the shoulder of a hill hid it from the watching crowds in the Gala Field.

Ten minutes later Lily plummeted to her death in a field close by Ponden Reservoir, next to the old Scar Top Refreshment Rooms, but exactly how it happened remains a mystery. An eyewitness, Robert Rushworth, watching through field-glasses from the nearby village of Stanbury, saw Lily leap from the balloon, her parachute only partly opened, then she and the parachute parted company while she was still about forty feet from the ground. She was wearing her harness and could only have unhooked herself from the parachute with the greatest of difficulty. Was the harness faulty, or could it have been tampered with? If so, it would most certainly have come to light when it was inspected later on, but nothing was suggested to that effect. Captain Bidmead had himself checked the harness before the ascent, and it was the one Lily had used many times before.

Mr Rushworth said he saw her 'shrugging her shoulders' as she left the balloon, but didn't see her raise her arms to the hooks. Another eyewitness, Mr Cowling Heaton, the 'refreshment housekeeper' at Scartop, said he saw Lily fall 'head over heels like a cartwheel' to her death.

Lily lived only brief minutes after the fall, and Cowling Heaton was the first to reach her, racing through the buttercups and long grass to kneel by her side. Captain Bidmead, who had followed the course of the balloon down the country lanes in a pony and trap, was next on the scene, closely followed by Charlie Merrall in his new-fangled motor car. By the time Doctor Thomson arrived to examine her she was dead from multiple injuries and shock, and shortly afterwards a covered wagon passed slowly through Stanbury on its way to Haworth, bearing the battered body of Lily Cove.

In the Gala Field in Haworth the crowds still waited for the triumphant return of Lily, who had promised she would come back to celebrate, and when they sighted Charlie Merrall's car entering the field a great cheer went up. They thought he was bringing the heroine home in triumph – instead, he brought news of her death.

At the inquest on Lily, where a verdict of accidental death was recorded, Captain Bidmead put forward a possible explanation that Lily had allowed herself to float too far before she jumped from the balloon. When they arrived in Haworth they had walked across the moors to see the course the balloon would take and had selected the field that Lily was to land in. When asked if Lily had made the descent at the proper time, Bidmead replied, 'She went further than she should. My instructions were that she should drop just over by the mill. If she had done so I should have been with her in a couple of minutes.' He thought that as she approached the Reservoir she might have panicked (she was a non-swimmer and notoriously afraid of water), misjudged her height (although the balloon was fitted with an aneroid which should have registered this) and made her fatal jump. Somehow she had managed to unhook herself from the parachute so as to avoid entanglement if she landed in the water.

Bidmead also told the inquest that the two of them were meant to appear at the Keighley Gala on the following Saturday. 'I intended her to have a quiet week's holiday in Keighley before Saturday. She was a jolly girl – she had a joke and a jest for everyone.'

From the inquest a recommendation was forwarded to the Home Secretary that 'performances of such dangerous exhibitions be discontinued by Act of Parliament or otherwise'. It was noted that their 'attraction to the public lies in the danger, not the achievement, and should be stopped in the interests of public morality'.

On the day of Lily's funeral Mr Fell, MP for Great Yarmouth, asked the Home Secretary, in Parliament, whether he did indeed intend to take steps to prohibit such 'exhibitions' in future, and Mr Gladstone replied that he was shortly hoping to introduce a bill extending the Dangerous Performances Acts to all women, whatever their age. Up to that time the Acts had covered only females up to the age of eighteen, and Lily Cove was the fourth recorded lady aeronaut to have met a tragic end.

The solution to the mystery of Lily Cove's death lies buried with her in the little cemetery on the edge of the moors at Haworth, within sight of the field where she met her death.

Her father, Thomas Cove, a poor man, was brought up from London for the funeral, and his 'decent' black suit was paid for by Captain Bidmead. Once more the crowds gathered, and many of the ladies were allowed a final glimpse of the dead face, after the custom of the times. The Rector of Haworth, the Revd T.W. Story, conducted a short service for relatives and close friends at the White Lion, and then the coffin, made of pitch pine and with heavy brass mountings, was carried in relays by members of the Haworth Gala Committee along the moor road to the cemetery. Albert Best was among those who headed the procession. Behind the coffin came a carriage and in it were Lily's father, Captain Bidmead, and several friends. In the cortège were members of the Haworth and Oxenhope Nursing Association and a private carriage of the Merrall family, and hundreds of villagers and sympathisers walked alongside. All over Haworth shutters were closed and curtains drawn as the shocked residents paid tribute to Lily.

In the stone quarries overlooking the cemetery, workmen stood in silence with bared heads as the sad procession approached, and during the short committal, as the words 'Ashes to ashes, dust to dust' were read, it is recorded that the 'melodious piping of a lark was heard, sending forth its message of love and sympathy to those left behind in affliction'. Among the many wreaths was one of pink roses from Charlie Merrall, bearing the words, 'In deepest sympathy for a brave girl who lost her life in the cause of charity.' Another one, of wild flowers, was left by a little boy who never disclosed his identity. A sheet placed at the cemetery for donations to defray the funeral expenses was generously patronised and the tombstone, raised by public subscription, bears the words, 'In the midst of life we are in death'.

Ironically, the Haworth Gala Committee met in July of that year and decided to abandon the Haworth Gala for the following year – after all that, the response had been disappointing, the net proceeds amounting to only £17 6s. Six months later Charlie Merrall married an actress who was appearing in pantomime at the Alhambra Theatre, Bradford.

Today Lily Cove is for the most part forgotten, and her grave lies untended and

Lily Cove's grave in the cemetery on the edge of Haworth moor, overlooking the route of her last balloon flight. On the stone is a carving of her balloon, showing the parachute fastened to one side of the mesh.

neglected. Dry leaves gather and whisper on it and lichens creep over the stone on which a faithful replica of the balloon and parachute she used is reproduced. The stone quarries nearby are now forever silent, but the larks still sing above the grave of this 'liberated' lady and tragic heroine.

5

Way of the Worth

The River Worth is born in Lancashire, offspring of the Watersheddles Reservoir which collects water from the surrounding moors to supply the Worth Valley and Keighley. Here the moors are at their bleakest – sheep wander at will across the unfenced road and the call of the red grouse and the curlew are carried on the wind.

But once over the summit, past the old Herders' Inn on its cliff top (now sadly closed for residential development), and looking into Lancashire towards Laneshaw Bridge, Wycoller and the Forest of Trawden (no longer forested), the Colne Valley seems green and fertile by comparison, with the great hump of Pendle Hill blocking the skyline. From the Yorkshire side of the watershed the land dips down to the Worth Valley.

Around Watersheddles itself there is just heather, peat and bog – and a great sense of freedom and space. The Brontë Way, a route for walkers between Haworth and Wycoller, adds almost a note of incongruity with its well-made stiles and attractive notice-boards.

Strange stones are dotted about the moors, relics of primitive formation or mystic past. Just north of the reservoir, 'Wolfstones' heaves itself on to the horizon like the broken prow of a ship, and on Crow Hill towards the south, and not visible from the reservoir, stands 'The Lad', a tall, pointed, rough-hewn stone with strange chiselled lettering:

LAD
ORSCARR
ON CROW
HILL

The 'O' in orscarr might well be a 'C', which makes it even more difficult to understand. 'The Lad' stands on the

Alcomden Stones, thought by many to be of druidical origin, swathed in bilberry bushes, on the high moors above Ponden Kirk.

Lancashire and Yorkshire boundary and as 'lad' in Scandinavian means boundary stone, there might be nothing more to it than that. A local story, fitting in with the mood of the moors, is much more interesting. It is said that the body of a lad was found there a long time ago, he having apparently succumbed while walking on the moors in a snowstorm. Nobody came forward to claim him and there was a dispute between Lancashire and Yorkshire as to who should bury him, the place where he was found being then just inside Yorkshire. Eventually Lancashire said they would do the decent thing – on condition that their boundary was pushed back to include the place where the lad was found. This story may not be true, but it certainly adds to the spirit of the place. Beyond 'The Lad', and above Ponden Kirk, are Alcomden Stones, druid in appearance – and who knows what happened on these moors in the distant past? It was around here that the Crow Hill Bog Burst took place in 1824, causing a torrent of yellow slime to erupt and course down the length of the Worth Valley, uprooting trees and inspiring a hell-fire sermon from Patrick Brontë.

From Watersheddles the river makes its peaceful way down a narrow, bracken-covered ravine which gradually widens and becomes more lush, passing old farms with evocative names – Silver Hill, Old Snap (the original home of the Heatons), Whitestone – and so to Ponden. Just before it enters the reservoir an old, double-arched bridge straddles it, carrying the Pennine Way as it drops from Wuthering Heights and then climbs the hills again to Cowling.

Signs of winter visitors – tracks of Canada geese in the ice and snow of Ponden Reservoir.

Now the Worth loses its identity briefly in this liquid asset of the Yorkshire Water Authority and the valley is generous and wide, looking down to Stanbury and Haworth. At the western end of the reservoir stands Ponden Hall with its grey cluster of outbuildings and what remains of the avenue of trees that was submerged when the reservoir was built. At one time the Hall was busy with the comings and goings of the Heaton family but now it has a dreamlike quality as it stands serenely on its green spur of land. Behind it is Ponden Clough, leading to Ponden Kirk, Emily Brontë's 'Penistone Crag', a mighty portcullis hung against the moors.

In summer the reservoir is alive with sailing boats and wind-surfers, but in winter the ice makes ominous creaking sounds against the embankment, loud enough to disturb those who live in the cottages close by. One of these cottages, next to the field where Lily Cove met her tragic end in 1906, used to be the old Scar Top Refreshment Rooms and when, traditionally, 'they used to walk in swarms from Lancashire to Haworth at Easter time', the ham and egg teas served up there would fortify them for the homeward journey.

Canada geese have made their home on the banks of the reservoir, and fly up the valley in wonderful formation, but each spring they disappear to less accessible mud-flats to renovate their plumage. They always return to plague the farmers nearby who say they are like an army of lawnmowers and eat up all their grass. Wild mink have been spotted, dark-coated descendants of some who staged a mass break-out from a mink farm in the valley many years ago.

Tranquillity at Ponden – with Whitestone Farm on the left and Owl Snape (known as 'Old Snap') on the right.

Long before that, a navvy encampment covered the area, which was likened to the Wild West as work went ahead on the building of the reservoir, and an old man remembers being told that little boys were paid to collect handfuls of small, grey worms from freshly dug trenches for the navvies, who ate them with gusto, still wriggling – protein on the hoof, so to speak.

Not far from the old Refreshment Rooms is tiny Scartop Chapel, famous for its 'Coppin'-on Charity'. Like many Yorkshire chapels built on a hill, it is much taller at the back (where it looks over the reservoir overflow and the goit to the old cotton mill) than it is at the front. Much would be said at the chapel, no doubt, when the brewery across the road, owned by the Heatons of Ponden Hall, was in full production, at the time the reservoir was built – the thirst of the navvies was apparently unquenchable. However, the chapel has outlasted the brewery, which is now barely a ruin by the roadside.

Across the reservoir embankment from Scar Top stands Rush Isles Farm. During the reservoir construction it was the home of the 'surgeon' or 'bone-setter' (nowadays known as 'quack'), whom the locals and navvies often visited with their ailments in preference to a trained doctor. Bone settings were done without anaesthetic and things could be made decidedly unpleasant for the 'difficult' patient. Remedies and recipes were bought from others in the fraternity, and some were quite hair-raising. The urine of a red cow, set to a jelly, was considered efficacious for the treatment of cancer, and the grime from a copper kettle added to a glass of brandy would cure a sore throat. For boils and carbuncles, take the yellow moss from old walls, boil it in fresh butter, strain while hot, and apply twice daily, and a simple cure for toothache was to sear out the root with a red-hot wire – an operation claimed to be painless for those brave enough to try it out. There's a lot to be said for these old cures. Many years ago an old lady healed a massive carbuncle of mine by slapping household soap and sugar on it under a lint dressing!

From Ponden Reservoir, the River Worth, escaping through an overflow, runs parallel to the mill race, or goit, that served the cotton mill established by the Heatons. Now Ponden Mill is once more in the textile business, selling household linens at competitive prices, as well as caneware and gifts. The open-air services for 'T'Coppin'-on Charity' were held in what is now a car park at Ponden Mill, in the days when wagonettes brought crowds to join in the hearty singing and hear hell-fire sermons. The services are still held, but the crowds are fewer, and the successor to the wagonette, the motor coach, brings customers to the Mill for retail therapy instead.

From Ponden the river enters the little, forgotten valley between Oldfield and Stanbury. The tops of the hills are pitted with disused quarries and coal-mines; lower down the slopes sheep and cattle feed in pleasant fields, and wildlife feels safe in the comparative calm. Herons have made this stretch their home, rising slowly on leaden wings if they are disturbed. The glint of a kingfisher can be seen, squirrels play in the trees, and in the night owls call plaintively through the stillness. The valley is alive with birds and in winter they strip the trees – holly, rowan, hawthorn – of their berries. In early spring the cuckoo calls and the silver sheen of pussy willow is rich

The young River Worth in a 'little forgotten valley' – looking over to Oldfield from Stanbury.

against grey water or dark ruins. In Maytime the slopes and fields are clothed in white blossom and bright with flowers. In early winter the valley is at its most dramatic as stark silhouettes of trees, grey stone walls and old farmhouses stand against a backdrop of moors painted in muted ochre, grey, orange, deep dark shades of green, and black. Later the east wind blows the snow horizontally against the farmhouse windows and the valley becomes a bowl of swirling whiteness.

By the ruins of Griffe Mill is a large green 'doughnut', its sides knitted with brambles, where the gasometer stood that lit the mill, while yet another overgrown goit leads into a disused dam behind the mill and trees grow where the looms and the water-wheel clattered not all that long ago. Just below the mill a small arch can be seen in the river bank where the tail goit, 'discarded' water from the wheel, flowed underground to join the river.

Down the river flows, past 'The Old Gentleman's Grave', where James Mitchell, 'late Proprietor and Occupier of Oldfield House', rests in his chosen place, and on to Lumb Foot and another ruined mill. Here two rows of cottages have been restored, as well as the larger house where the overlooker lived. In the early nineteenth century the mill was owned by the Butterfield family of Cliffe Castle, Keighley, and was a flourishing place, being enlarged several times. It boasted a blacksmith's shop and one of the best bands in the area. Now, in spite of the renovated cottages, or perhaps because of them, Lumb Foot has no identity, being almost entirely taken over by very large and very smelly farm buildings and an abundance of old car tyres. From here a good track goes up the side of the valley to Stanbury and opposite a path goes up to Pickles Hill.

New arrivals on a Worth Valley hill farm, Stanbury.

The river is soon past Lumb Foot. Looking back towards Stanbury a statuesque group of pine trees tops the gradual rise of the hill towards the village cemetery, and then the ridge flattens out for the village itself.

Soon the Worth is joined by the Sladen Beck and they choose their meeting-place well, at Long Bridge, an old pack-horse bridge, and here a ford also crosses the river. To add to its busyness, comparatively speaking at least, an old track that was once well used comes down from Haworth and crosses the valley to Pickles Hill.

Past Long Bridge, with Haworth on its hill and the road leading to the moors, Springhead Mills still stand, where folk from Stanbury and Oldfield used to walk down the valley daily to their work. Now the mill has been converted into a modern housing development.

The greenness of the Upper Worth Valley is left behind now – instead the river comes to a welter of fords, bridges, goits and sluices and finally to the railway near Vale Mills in a gigantic game of leapfrog. 'Worth Valley Railway' it may be called, but for the second half of its journey from Keighley to Oxenhope it has actually left the Worth Valley proper and is steaming by the side of the Oxenhope Beck. It was at Vale Mills, built at the start of the worsted boom but now devoted to plastics and printing, that the railway crossed the mill dam on a rickety trestle viaduct. The viaduct was pulled down about twenty-five years after the railway opened, and the mill dam is now a car park.

At Vale Mills we see something of the 'eternal triangle' between the railway, the beck and the river. Coming down from Oxenhope by the side of the beck, the train emerges from Mytholmes Tunnel and sees the River Worth. At the same time the beck and the Worth join forces, but with the river keeping the upper hand and name, and they coyly disappear under Vale Mills itself, leaving the railway to find its own way to Oakworth Station.

Finally, near Oakworth Station, there is reconciliation, and the River Worth and the railway run companionably down the Worth Valley to Keighley. Its green valley is far behind it now – the River Worth is surrounded by industry, noise and dirt, and it finally drowns its sorrows in the wider waters of the River Aire.

6

Lament for the Brontë Bus

A s the bus rattled to a halt in the windswept village street and the passengers started to clamber aboard, a cottage door was flung open and an urgent headful of curlers peered out.

'Can you manage to wait for George – he's no'an finished shaving yet?' After a reassuring wave from the driver the curlers withdrew and the passengers settled down for a chat until George finally appeared, fresh-faced and beaming, to take his seat.

The time was nothing like the present, the occasion an everyday occurrence in the life of a not-very-everyday enterprise – the Brontë Bus Company of Haworth, which at one time provided the villages of Stanbury, Oxenhope and Laneshaw Bridge with a regular bus service, as well as being synonymous with choir trips, Sunday School treats, and outings for every church, chapel and club in the area.

Innumerable songs were composed by choirboys and concert parties about the Brontë Buses, and always they were sung with affection. The hallmark of the company was service to the passenger – clogs, meat and other necessities of life were willingly collected in Haworth and dropped off at the appropriate door in Stanbury for a penny or tuppence (in those halcyon days before we went 'decimal'), milk cans were picked up from farms for delivery to Haworth Station, credit was extended to 'regulars' who had forgotten their purses, and although 'Could you just drop me off at Uncle Joe's?' sometimes meant a slight detour, service was carried out with a smile.

In all weathers the Brontë Bus could be relied upon to get through when nothing else could, its boot filled with ashes and its driver equipped with a spade – although there was one never-to-be-forgotten winter when the deep snow, drifted at the top of the switchback known as Sladen Bridge between Haworth and Stanbury, was just too much for it, and the bus was completely buried for three days.

Flexibility was another characteristic of Brontë Buses. In the days when the Kirkstone Pass in the Lake District presented a serious obstacle to all drivers, a choir trip from Hawksbridge Chapel set out for Patterdale, and it was a perspiring driver who landed his charges at their destination. 'You don't expect me to go back over that there mountain, do you?', he asked them in agony of mind. 'Nay lad, don't thee worry thisel',' came back the answer, 'we can go back home be Keswick' – and so they did.

Model T Ford fourteen-seater wagon, first vehicle of the Brontë Bus Company. With solid tyres and canvas 'curtains' round the sides it doubled as a haulage wagon – 'but it was transport'. (Reproduced courtesy of Peter and Michael Snaith)

Not only that, having arrived at Keswick, two small organ blowers, firmly holding to the belief that, offered an inch one should hold out stoutly for a yard, expressed a wish to go home via Morecambe. Which they did, and the whole party enjoyed an hour by the seaside before they turned homewards.

But flexibility can also have its drawbacks. Another church, at Ingrow, annually arranged a trip to Morecambe for its young choristers. In those days travel was rare, and as the route happened to pass the house of an old friend of the choirmaster, that gentleman always took the opportunity of stopping the bus and calling in to renew old acquaintance. With the journey barely begun, while he sipped tea and reminisced, thirty angry young faces watched powerless from the bus windows as visions of sea, dodgems and penny slot-machines receded further and further as the minutes ticked by.

The Brontë Bus Company was in effect founded in 1924 when John Snaith and Maurice Taylor went into partnership in a small garage at Lees, Crossroads, and also ran a local taxi service. So numerous were the requests for transport to Stanbury, and even for a regular bus service, that they eventually decided to comply and on Friday night, 8 December 1926, the first Brontë service bus ran between Haworth and Stanbury.

It was a modest vehicle, an old Model T Ford fourteen-seater wagon, bought for £30, and with its wooden top and canvas sides it did double duty as a haulage wagon. On its first journey the fares collected amounted to 3*s* 9*d* and petrol was 1*s* a gallon. The only form of lighting inside the old wagon was a bicycle lamp, and comfort was secondary. 'When you got on in the dark you didn't know whose knee you were sitting on – but it was transport,' recollected an old Stanbury villager, Mrs Gladys Shackleton.

In 1928 Mr Taylor and Mr Snaith dissolved their partnership, Mr Taylor taking over the garage side of the business and Mr Snaith the transport – there was by now a flourishing bus service operating between Haworth and Stanbury. The first bus in the morning arrived in Stanbury in time to get the workers to the mills in Haworth for 6 a.m. – it also saw the last of the shift workers back to Stanbury at 10 o'clock each night, which meant that the drivers sometimes worked an eighteen-hour day. Mrs Shackleton maintained that the village 'was never better bussed' than in those days, and that the Brontë Buses and excellent Co-operative Society were the life-blood of the village.

The old Ford T wagon was eventually replaced by a Fiat bus bought from the Harrogate Carriage Company for the grand sum of £80. Unfortunately, the bodywork protruded somewhat over the back wheels and the steep gradient of Sladen Bridge

Fiat bus with protruding rear end . . . no good on a steep gradient! (Reproduced courtesy of Peter and Michael Snaith)

almost proved its undoing. On one momentous trip, everything and everybody slithered to the back of the vehicle and the front wheels rose majestically into the air. No one was hurt, the incident was taken in good part by everybody concerned, and an eyewitness praised the behaviour of the 'cool and competent driver'. Another favourite vehicle from the early days was 'Old Bill', a Ford fourteen-seater with a 'jumbo' gearbox – seven forward and seven reverse gears. Admittedly you could have walked faster when it was in bottom gear, but it was ideal for driving up Main Street with a full load.

In the old days Haworth Main Street in wintry weather was something akin to a toboggan run, and the best thing for scattering was old-fashioned ashes from the mill boilers. When the old boilers were replaced by the oil-fired variety, the company had to rely on sand and grit, which was considered to be not half so efficient when it came to providing a grip on icy roads.

Early winter mornings in Haworth Main Street could be particularly difficult, but a knock on the door of a gentleman called Albert Wilson who lived in Old Piccadilly (an area of Main Street now demolished), and who worked for the Corporation, would ensure that the street would be ashed before the bus returned from Stanbury with its first load of workers at 6 a.m.

The Corporation always left grit at the top of Sladen Bridge for the bad weather, but of course difficulties occurred long before the bus could reach the top. Nothing daunted, the bus driver would borrow a barrow from a nearby farmer and cart the

'Old Bill', a Ford fourteen-seater with a 'jumbo' gearbox: slow but sure on hills. (Reproduced courtesy of Peter and Michael Snaith)

A Commer fourteen-seater bought new in 1929. On one occasion the seats were taken out and the entire Snaith family went off and had a holiday in Torquay in it. The ladies slept in the bus, the chaps in a tent. 'I remember – we all sat on buffets' (stools). (Reproduced courtesy of Peter and Michael Snaith)

grit where it was needed. Both Sladen Bridge and Main Street were responsible for phenomenal bills for petrol and brake linings, but the Brontë Bus Company took it all in its stride!

Saturday nights were busy nights when two 'picture buses' waited for Haworth's two cinemas to 'loose' and then transported picture-goers back home to Oxenhope and Stanbury. And they didn't return empty; last-minute revellers were picked up from local hostelries, the bus driver sometimes having to go inside said hostelry and, with a loud cry of 'bus!', round up his recalcitrant flock.

One long-ago summer a group of ladies from Hawksbridge Chapel was booked to perform a play, written by one of their number, at remote Crimshaw Dene. Of course a Brontë Bus was booked for the occasion and turned up promptly in the early evening to convey thespians and supporters. Nothing, however, would induce the bus to start, in spite of the united efforts of players and friends in pushing. An old van and a couple of cars were summoned to convey the artists, their supporters staying behind to give any further assistance that was needed. Eventually the company sent another bus and the supporters arrived in time for the second half of the performance, which had to be completed 'before the sun went down', there being no adequate form of lighting in Crimshaw Dene chapel at that time. Indeed, the performance was part of a scheme to raise money to install that new-fangled thing called gas lighting!

A 'fleet' of Brontë buses in the early thirties. Left to right – Commer Invader, Commer fourteen-seater and Chevrolet – parked at Dimples Quarry, Haworth. (Reproduced courtesy of Peter and Michael Snaith)

As well as the local bus service, day excursions, school transport and factory services kept the firm busy, and at the local holiday week a dozen Brontë Buses lined up to take people to Blackpool, Morecambe, Bridlington or Scarborough. Eventually sons Michael and Peter joined John Snaith in the family business. Its heyday was immediately after the last world war, when the company ran thirteen coaches, and Brontë Tours even reached as far as the continent, but in 1956 the local bus service to the villages was taken over by the West Yorkshire Bus Company – travel in the area ceased to be an occasion and became simply a means of getting from A to B.

From then on things became more and more difficult for this unique little bus company. Maintenance and renewal costs rose steeply, legislation regarding working hours was frustrating, the local textile industry declined, more people had their own cars, and numerous chapels in the area closed down, with the result that bookings for day trips diminished. Also, more and more people started to book package deals for holidays abroad, and vandalism at sports fixtures made coach trips there a hazard.

Finally, in January 1981, Brontë Tours closed down and another chapter was over in the life of the Worth Valley. But at the little chapels and churches that still flourish up and down the valley, and in the hearts of the older residents, there will be happy memories of trips and excursions when the Brontë Bus Company provided a service that was more than a service – it was part of a way of life that is fast disappearing.

7

A Windmill at Newsholme

The hamlet of Newsholme stands sturdily on the slopes of the Yorkshire Pennines, about a mile from the Lancashire border. A signpost on the way from Oakworth says 'Newsholme. No through road', and at first glance it might seem that time has indeed stood still there. Its old millstone grit buildings blend harmoniously into the landscape, and it has an air of peaceful permanence. But although Newsholme's history goes back to the Domesday survey, when it is recorded that 'in the Berewick of Newhouse William had one carucate (about 110 acres) to be taxed', its feet are firmly planted in the twentieth century.

The first thing you notice as you approach Newsholme is a windmill, like some giant metal daisy, growing out of Church Farm, the home of David and Betty Ogden. David, whose family have lived at Church Farm since 1880, in addition to his farming enjoys making gadgets to improve farm equipment, and his windmill is the culmination of much thought and experiment. Now, 'in a windy winter', it can save up to £5 a week in electricity by warming water for the milking parlour and providing light for the garages.

The inscription carved over the door of Church Farm is RH–SH 1670. Robert Hall was a yeoman farmer (the SH is lost in the mist of history) who, having built his house at Newsholme, settled down to farming and becoming one of the pillars of the church at Keighley, to which parish Newsholme belonged at that time. All went well until Robert and Rector Miles Gail had a bust-up of tremendous proportions and uncertain origin, whereupon Robert transferred his allegiance to Skipton Church, some 9 miles away.

Newsholme once had two bobbin mills, and for a long time the lower one was the home of the Laycock family. Standing by a picturesque stream, with power derived from its water-wheel, it made and repaired bobbins, farm implements and small items of cottage furniture, and many a new bride in the district 'set up' with bread board, rolling-pin and a strange solid potato masher made at Newsholme bobbin mill. It was no uncommon sight in long spells of dry weather to see horses and carts backed into the small dam to allow the water to expand the wooden cartwheels and so prevent the metal rims from falling off.

Not only did the bobbin mill provide the community with employment and equipment – it was also the local gossip corner and meeting-place, that most

Church Farm, Newsholme, with its windmill – a pioneer at that time. On the roof to the left the tiny bell-tower can be seen on the church section.

necessary of all country institutions. That is, until one of the sons got a girl 'in t'family way'. The eldest brother, choirmaster of Oakworth Church, felt the disgrace keenly, and forbade further loitering at the bobbin mill forthwith. 'There'll be no more gossiping here', was the taciturn comment of the head of the Laycock family.

Another master of the bobbin mill, locally known as 'Old Jonie', took upon himself the job of watchdog of the local lads. Those that were courting 'away' had to pass the bobbin mill on their way home and 'Old Jonie' kept a careful check on the time everybody turned in.

One lad, wishing to teach the old man a lesson, went home across the fields, climbing over walls where necessary, and when he arrived home he went to bed without putting on the lights. On his way to work the following morning he was accosted by 'Old Jonie', full of righteous anger. 'Nah then, ye so-and-so, tha nivver come 'ome at all last neet. Tha owt to be ashamed o' thissen.' 'Ow dost t'a know?' asked the lad innocently. 'Ah know 'cos Ah waited up 'til half past two for thee, that's ow Ah know,' returned the tired old man.

In recent times there has been an influx of 'off-comed 'uns' into Newsholme, most of them commuting to places like Leeds during the day, but they have welded into the community, and the children, particularly, are giving the hamlet a new lease of life. The Ogdens have installed modern equipment, including a complete farming complex, and are keeping well abreast of the times. Indeed, they are almost ahead of them, thanks to David's gadgets. New barns are being built – partly because some of the old ones have been converted into dwelling-houses for the newcomers.

In among all this upsurge Church Farm stands pretty well as it has done for hundreds of years – at the heart of Newsholme. The building itself is unique and serves a threefold purpose under one roof. At the west end is the church, consecrated as such in 1840. Now officially in the parish of Oakworth, it remains the property of the Ogden family, and trustees are required to pay David all of one shilling (5p) rent per year. For this sum, David is responsible for all the external painting and renovating – the church trustees being responsible for the inside. There is a clause in the deeds to the effect that if the church remains empty for six months it will revert to being a working part of the farm again – an interesting situation which seems unlikely to crop up!

At one corner of the church is a quaint chimney, completely covered in ivy, the outward and visible sign of an antiquated heating system which was in operation until fairly recently. This consisted of an underfloor boiler which simply warmed the air before it escaped through a grille in the floor in front of the chancel. So efficient could this system be that it has been known for the grille to glow red hot – thus adding weight to John Bunyan's assertion that 'there is a path to hell, even from the gates of heaven', and even on less spectacular Sundays the shoes of unsuspecting visiting preachers have been seen to be smoking as they passed 'twixt vestry and pew.

Unfortunately, some might feel, the old boiler has been replaced by much more predictable and mundane storage heaters, and today's preachers are less likely to be set on fire than were their predecessors.

The windows of the church are all plain glass so that the surrounding fields seem, most appropriately, to be part of the worship, and each Rogation Day the congregation walks round the fields in the time-honoured custom. On a sunny day strange flickers can be observed playing on the inside walls of the church – it is the sun catching the metal blades of David's windmill and in turn being reflected through the windows.

Hanging loose at the back of the church and dangling in a tantalising way within easy reach over the back pew is the single bell rope – a source of great temptation to generations of small boys and a constant source of worry to their mothers!

The central part of the building is the farm itself, where a beautiful wrought-iron staircase, the work of David, blends with old oak beams and stone windows and passages. An outline of the old inglenook fireplace can be seen, but the recess has been filled in and a more functional stone fireplace takes its place. On a Sunday morning anyone at the farm not attending church can still join in the hymn-singing which drifts from 'next door' but, alas, the sound of Grandad whistling in his workshop in accompaniment to the sermon is just a memory.

The third part of the building is the Sunday School, and it is here that the socials are held which are famous throughout the district. Traditional homemade meat and potato pie suppers, and that good old favourite, pie and peas, are still on the menu. 'The Socials are something like an Outward Bound course,' says Betty Ogden wryly, 'but people seem to like them. In fact, they always come back again and even bring their friends.'

All the old games are played, to suit all ages, and everybody joins in. The little coke stove in the corner, which seemed inadequate at the start of the evening, gets dampened down to its lowest as enthusiasm mounts, and windows are flung open to revive flagging energy and let in the cool night air.

The noise of the social and the fun and games drifts down towards the old bobbin mill, now a dwelling-house, but with its water-wheel renovated and working again, and Cuckoo Beck meanders aimlessly through the reeds and meadows.

But above Church Farm David's windmill stands proudly against the night sky, making use of every wind of change – just like the hamlet of Newsholme itself.

8

Coppin'-on at Ponden

And what is 'coppin'-on'? Well may you ask! T'Coppin'-on Charity takes place every second Sunday in June when tiny Scar Top Chapel, about two miles from Haworth, celebrates its anniversary. Normally held in the open air, it used to be the highlight of the year in the valley. Literally thousands converged on foot, on horse and in wagonettes to hear hell-fire preachers, hearty singing and brass bands, and every home and farm in the area was open for hospitality.

Crowds assembling in their Sunday best for Scar Top Charity, 1915. Traditionally held in the open air at nearby Ponden Mill the congregation spilled over and up the hillsides to listen to hell-fire preachers and brass bands. And that's where the 'coppin'-on' came in!

Some of the sermons were lengthy and the young folk would take the opportunity, while their elders' minds were engaged on higher things, to wander off in pairs along the little streams and cloughs. Romance, as well as redemption, was very much in the air, and many a long-established state of wedded bliss in and around the Worth Valley owes its origins to Scar Top Anniversary.

During the break between afternoon and evening services, while refreshments were served in the chapel and farmhouse tables groaned under the weight of home baking, families were reunited, old friendships renewed and snippets of local gossip exchanged. One old bachelor in Stanbury who existed mainly on porridge was known to bake but twice a year – once at Christmas and once 'for t'Charity'.

After it was all over, and peace settled once more on the valley, one of the topics of conversation, no doubt, was who had 'copped-on', paired off, clicked, call it what you will, at the Anniversary.

It was in 1818 that Scar Top was built, and the original inscription on the outside of the building read 'Stanbury and Oakworth General Sunday School, built by subscription on the principles of Union and Philanthropy. Anno Domini 1818'. The land was bought from John Wright of Oakworth for £6, stone was cut from nearby quarries and all the construction work was done by local people in their spare time. The building was also used as a chapel, with sixteen trustees, and the Methodists soon took over the running of the Sunday School 'by permission'.

In 1869 a storm blew up in the valley when it was decided to rebuild the chapel. A Building Committee was formed of four trustees and five members of the Sunday School Committee, the old building was demolished – and the Building Committee asked permission of the trustees to erect a new inscription stone. (By strange chance the old one had been broken and some said it was no accident!) The new one was to read 'Wesleyan Chapel, built 1818, rebuilt 1869'. The trustees were incensed, considering this 'false, dishonest and illegal'; the storm spread down the valley to Keighley, where it was taken up by the local press, and to this day the inscription stone above the door of the chapel is a non-committal blank.

The storm soon abated, goodwill prevailed and t'Charity continued to prosper, sometimes attracting as many as two and three thousand. The band, drawn from nearby chapels, played with verve and versatility on instruments such as the hautboy, clarinet, bass-viol, fiddle, cornopean, serpent, flageolet, ophicleide and bombardon (some of these are now only to be found in museums), and their efforts did not go unnoted. Over a hundred years ago 'Will Feather with his trombone as clean as a pin and as breet as silver, with his black coat and white waistcoat, checked trousers, and particularly clean himself' was one of the players.

Famous names came to Scar Top, preachers, singers and conductors, and John Heaton, one of the 'five brethren' of Ponden Hall, was choirmaster for forty-five years, composing special hymns and anthems for the chapel.

Wholeheartedness is a hallmark of the valley folk, and the central purpose of the Charity was praise and thanksgiving. The singing and playing could be heard for miles, blown by the moorland breeze and mingling with the sound of birdsong and the young River Worth.

Scar Top Chapel, near Ponden: 'Built by subscription on the principles of Union and Philanthropy.'

The collection was also important, for it helped to maintain the chapel through the year (perhaps the word 'charity' comes from the fact that folk were expected to dig deep), and great was the rivalry between Scar Top and Stanbury Chapels in this respect. Scar Top had the advantage in that their Charity came last and they knew the record they had to beat, and it was also in the open air. This meant that the stewards could comb the hillsides, where the crowds perched in their Sunday best like flocks of bright birds, and call at any farms that might have folk still at home. They were even known to station themselves at strategic points on the road to take advantage of passing traffic.

The trustees of the chapel met monthly and took their duties seriously, at one time being fined 1*s* for missing a meeting. They were also, apparently, very obliging, as their minutes record that 'Charlie Moore be allowed to take the harmonium home to practise for the Charity'.

Although the Charity was the main annual event, Scar Top played a vital part in the life of the valley generally. Built at a time when the face of Britain was changing fast, it provided stability and continuity – surnames appearing in the first registers can still be found in the valley today. There was the Scar Top 'Stir', or social evening, when the local grocer took his goods round to the ladies for baking, and they would think nothing of producing 400 buns at a time, while on one occasion it was decided that 'Mary Barker should be asked to warm the sad cakes and two men be appointed to collect them from her cottage'. Sad cakes were similar to teacakes, but made with suet. The Stirs were usually held when there was a full moon, as this was the only illumination along the country roads at that time.

Elizabeth Snowden attended the Sunday School as a little girl a century ago and once told me about the annual Walking Day, a red-letter occasion, with marching and singing, a tea, sports in the evening – and an extended bed-time. The scholars were presented with three Victoria plums 'picked at point of perfection', and a little triangular bag of baked sweets 'of every conceivable shape and texture, in gentle pastel colours' – nothing so blatant as pear drops or humbugs.

Sunday School was a meeting-place for all the local children, where punctuality was paramount – those paragons who were in their places at the start could cheerfully reply 'In time' when the roll was called, but late-comers must answer with a shamefaced 'Present'. Nothing else was said, but the guilt was keenly felt. In times past the Sunday School had given reading lessons, and emphasis was still on reading aloud in unison, boys and girls suitably separated, while the small non-readers looked at picture books. The floor was hard for kneeling on, but Elizabeth recalled that there were no concessions to comfort, such as hassocks, during prayers.

Scar Top also played a big part in James Riley's life, and his father's before him, and his grandfather's (he was organist there), and James himself was a trustee for many years. At one time the stage for the band and preachers took nearly all Saturday to erect. 'We even had a plan of how to put it together.' Of course, on Monday night it didn't take quite so long to take down, and that was quite a get-together. 'We used to eat up all the food left from Sunday and send somebody to Haggate Nook for an ounce of twist for us all to share. The older ones chewed it and the rest just smoked it in clay pipes.' Indeed, days long gone.

At that time Haworth Band was the regular band, augmented by the more genteel Marsh Orchestra, but the conductor was always independent, to avoid ill-feeling. 'If t'Charity happened to fall at Whitsuntide, Haworth Band was busy with Whit Walks, so me and a mate used to set off on our bikes to round up a band from other chapels,' James told me.

Wartime rationing put a stop to hospitality as far as the chapel itself was concerned – it was restricted to drinks with own food with the full treatment only for the band and preacher. 'In the old days we always sang grace, and it was hectic if it rained and the services had to be held inside. With only the one room we had to deal with the tea in between the services.'

Times change. Several years ago the local Methodist Circuit, to which Scar Top paid its dues, tried to close it, along with other chapels in the area (Scar Top is still officially just a Sunday School), but Scar Top would not be closed. 'We weren't havin' no'an,' said George Bancroft, another trustee, and now Scar Top soldiers on alone, independent as it was originally planned to be. Indeed, I suspect it was ever a

Scar Top, with the chapel on the right, looking up from the low track past Ponden Mill to Ponden Reservoir.

law unto itself. It still holds its Charity on the second Sunday in June, and no doubt there is still a certain amount of 'coppin'-on', although the crowds are much smaller and the wagonettes are gone forever. But the singing and the playing are hearty as ever, and the preaching just as challenging, vying with the noise of the River Worth on one side and the internal combustion engine on the tourist track on the other.

The future of this small, brave chapel is uncertain, with most of its congregation elderly and not as many young people coming on. One thing is sure – if it has to close it will be a sad day, and the end of an era in the history of the Worth Valley.

9

Facts of Life and Death

Living conditions were appalling in Haworth when the Brontës arrived in 1820, and Patrick Brontë strove for years to have something done about them. Eventually, after much correspondence with the General Board of Health and a petition signed by 222 of the residents, Benjamin Herschel Babbage arrived in the village in 1850 to make a 'preliminary enquiry' into the situation. He, too, was horrified at what he saw.

At that time Haworth, described as a 'small triangular plot of houses, high upon the hill', consisted of 316 dwellings, 25 of them being cellar houses, although the steep hillsides dictated that the land would be higher on one side of the houses than on others.

There was not one water closet and 68 privies served the entire population – barely one privy to every 4½ houses. (The Brontës had their own private two-seater in the backyard.) Two of the privies used – by a dozen families each – were in the public street, not only within view of the houses but 'exposed to the gaze of passers-by'. Next to each privy, and against the house, stood a midden heap on which household refuse, slaughterhouse offal and 'night soil' were thrown. Often a pigsty stood close by and the seepage from this contributed to the general unsavoury mess. At the Druggist's house, opposite the Black Bull, the contents of the midden-heap often reached the sill of the larder window, and a woman living there complained that she could not eat because of the stench. The middens were cleared from time to time by local farmers and their contents thrown upon the fields, although the residue from the 'night soil' did nothing for the land. There were no sewers, few covered drains, and for the most part the sewage ran in open channels down the street. From the cesspit of one privy at the top of Main Street a 'disgusting effluvium' continually drained into the street and often the doors of the cesspit would burst open to deposit the entire contents into the street. Within two yards of this cesspit door was the pump which supplied drinking water to the people living around.

Water to this pump came through the churchyard just above it, which Babbage condemned as being badly drained and overcrowded. About 1344 burials had taken place there in the preceding ten years, and these burials alone should have covered the entire area of the churchyard. The gravestones were all laid flat, either directly over the ground or slightly raised on stones, thus preventing the entry of air into the

Overcrowded graves in Haworth old churchyard.

soil to assist decomposition, and so close together were they that no purifying grass could grow between or beneath them.

If the dead were deprived of space, so were the living. Large families were crammed into small houses and the overcrowded sleeping arrangements were most unhealthy. To make matters worse, many of the villagers did wool-combing in their cottages for the local mills and this often took place in the bedrooms. Stoves were

Old houses in Haworth, including Acton Street and Well Street, which were demolished in about 1970. They stood where the Changegate car park is now.

often installed to ensure the correct high temperature for the wool-combing, and windows were kept closed to preserve the heat. Consequently, many of the villagers slept in hot, unventilated, congested conditions where germs could abound.

Eleven water pumps served the villagers, and seven wells, although five of these were private. The more fastidious considered the pump water not suitable for drinking (it wasn't), and this often entailed a walk of more than half a mile to the nearest well, although in a hot summer the wells were scanty and putrid and in one case even the cows refused to drink the water.

About thirty-five of Haworth's houses were a little better served for water, thanks to the initiative of a gentleman called Mr Thomas, who had rented a spring called Sowden's Spring and drained it into a small cistern. From this, he laid pipes to the favoured few houses and charged them 3*s* to 5*s* a year for the service. The pipes and taps were leaky, and often those living at the end of the system could get no water if everybody else was using it, but nevertheless it was an improvement.

Not surprisingly among all this, dysentery, cholera and typhus, 'Low Fever', were rife, and the annual mortality rate was high – 25.4 per thousand. Average life expectancy was just under twenty-six years and the infant mortality rate under six years was 41.6 per cent.

In 1826 the Haworth Registers record the burials of eight members of one family, the Burwins, between the end of September and the beginning of December, and seven of them were below the age of twenty-five.

Conditions improved, but slowly, and the gravestones in Haworth churchyard are sadly eloquent. One of them, upright and only slightly more recent, is beautifully carved with fruit and flowers and at the base, beneath a carved canopy, an infant sleeps on a tasselled cushion, its head resting on a chubby arm. The gravestone was carved with great care by Joseph Heaton, a stonemason, and the lettering tells us that in the grave lie his seven infants, his wife Elizabeth and himself. The baby on the cushion is said to be a perfect likeness of his son, James Whitham, even down to the last dimple, and James was just one year old. Often in summer, bunches of wild flowers appear in the curved arms of the sleeping baby – put there by local children who sense something of the sad story. Joseph died in 1914 aged sixty-nine, victim of silicosis, and his wife Elizabeth followed him three years later, aged seventy-one – their epitaph reads 'Sweet Rest at Last'.

The grave of James Whitham Heaton, his six small brothers and sisters and his parents. The carving, done by his father, is said to be a likeness of James, and children often lay wild flowers in the baby's arms in summer.

Eventually the old churchyard was closed, Haworth was cleaned up, and water and sewage properly dealt with, but the past left its legacy in people's attitudes to mere mortality. Coffin boards, bidding cards and funeral biscuits with ham teas were just a part of the everyday scene in the early years of the last century, and death was simply a fact of life.

Two old men, Enoch and Jonas, lived on a small primitive farm just outside Haworth. Enoch was a lamplighter and his tools were a ladder and a box of matches. One day the local muffin man's son, Leslie Feather, came to the farm to deliver the weekly supply of oatcake. Finding nobody about, he draped the oatcake over the rack in the kitchen and was about to leave when he noticed something on the kitchen table covered with a sheet. Being an inquisitive lad he took a peep under the sheet and to his horror there was Enoch, laid out and definitely dead. He got out of the farm quickly, and just outside met Jonas on his way home. He stuttered his condolences and asked how it happened. 'Well,' replied Jonas, 'it were like this. Ah were asleep t'other neet in't bed and Ah woke up and, by, Ah felt cold. An' then Ah looked at 'im and theer 'e were – stone dead by t'side o' me.' Leslie was shocked. 'What on earth did you do?' he asked. 'Well, what could Ah do in't middle o't neet? Ah pushed 'im up into a corner and turned ower and went to sleep again,' explained Jonas.

But in most cases death has to be properly attended to, and Minnie Hey was just such an attendant. She was a shroud-maker and layer-outer who lived in Haworth at the turn of the last century, and her approach to her job was matter-of-fact, reflecting those times when chapels of rest were unheard of and men bared their heads as funerals passed slowly by. She kept newspaper cuttings about the deaths of her clients (including Lily Cove) and wore loose-fitting dentures, clogs and a hairnet. Of necessity she was thrifty; almost everything in her home was handmade, then eventually unpicked and remade, and her hands were never still – on the rare occasions when she sat down to rest, her thumbs were continually twiddling.

Minnie Hey, shroud-maker and 'layer-outer' in Haworth around the beginning of the twentieth century. She did what was necessary for Lily Cove after her tragic death in 1906. (Reproduced courtesy of Jean Medley)

If Minnie's cottage was austere (soft sandstone was crushed and laid weekly as the only floor covering), her coffins were comfortable. Layered with wood shavings, they were lined and decorated with fancy cord – after all, they were on show for all to see before the funeral.

Shrouds hung everywhere in her living-room and were even draped over the furniture – satin for oak coffins and muslin for pitch pine. Who said that death is the great leveller? They were works of art, decorated with tassels, covered buttons and bows, but pockets were deemed unnecessary. Each shroud was simply a fancy front, to be nailed to the sides of the coffin – backs were also thought irrelevant. 'If people were going anywhere, they certainly weren't coming back,' commented Donald Hey, Minnie's son.

Donald remembered gardening as a boy when 'Young Wood', Alfred, aged eighty-six, peered over the garden wall. 'Wheer's your mother? Tell her to come an' lig ar Billy art – he's just deed.' Billy, his brother, was ninety-six. 'You'd better go with me – Ah sall want a lift – it'll be a reet muck 'oil,' said Minnie when Donald took the message, so Donald went with her.

After helping to lift Billy, with his long white beard flowing across his chest, from the shut-up bed where he'd died, and sweeping all the 'dawn' from underneath it, Donald was sent to the joiner's shop run by the two brothers for the usual coffin board. 'It's in yon corner,' said Alfred, and Donald, surprised, saw a coffin already made. When he moved it he was even more surprised to see an identical coffin reared up behind it. 'We s'll want one apiece, won't we?' said Alfred, and lovingly stroked the good oak. 'Ye can't get wood like this easily these days, tha knows.' There's nothing like being prepared!

Time has moved on; life can now be both antiseptic and mundane, death seems to come as a sad surprise, and our acceptance of the inevitable is more reluctant. Perhaps we're missing something – after all, there's a certain amount of camaraderie to be enjoyed while sitting on a two-seater privy in a back yard.

10

Of Moles and Men

If the appearance of my garden is anything to go by (it resembles, in miniature, the slag-heap section of a busy colliery), then the mole population is definitely on the increase. I am also of the opinion that moles can read. Not long ago, returning from our holidays, we found a notice pinned to our dividing fence by the next door neighbour. 'Moles this way,' it said, with an arrow pointing in our direction. He said it was a joke, but I think the moles took it seriously.

It was a relief, therefore, to meet John Heaton while I was on a visit to Martha, his sister, at Hawksbridge, near Haworth, for John had been an honorary mole catcher for about forty years. 'Have you ever seen a mole trap?' he asked, coming into Martha's kitchen. I hadn't. 'Come outside then and have a look.' We went into John's niece's garden next door, where John had been at work. He had uncovered part of a mole 'run' to retrieve a trap, and its victim lay on the ground beside it. I was amazed at the strength and beauty of the pink forefeet and gently stroked the grey-brown velvet skin. John had used a 'barrel' trap, the type used in the area for many years, and as he stooped down to replace it in the 'run', he carefully flattened the ground round it with the dead mole. Apparently moles can detect soil disturbances very easily, and also have a keen sense of smell, quickly noticing alien odours like petrol, oil, soap, tobacco, which are transferred to the soil by the hands. They are also very curious. 'Just occasionally you get a mole caught in either end of a barrel trap. One goes in and squeaks as it's caught, then another comes along the other way and wonders what's the matter, so he pokes in as well,' explained John.

By this time I was fascinated by the subject of moles and went along to see John in his cottage a few days later. John was born and brought up at nearby Westfield Farm, like his father before him, and his grandfather came to live there at the age of eight.

Just behind Westfield is Upper Westfield, locally known as 'T'Drop' for a rather sinister reason. The story goes that a couple once lived there who'd come from 'Stair 'Oyle' above Marsh. They'd had a son, a backward lad, who'd given the game away when they'd been involved in some shady activity. The lad disappeared. Many years later a body was recovered from the moorland bog in a complete state of preservation and the inquest, held at a pub when the body was exhibited, aroused

John Heaton with mole – 'four (skins) make a lovely pair of insoles for wellies in cold weather'.

much interest. All this happened well over a hundred years ago – the inquest and the body are fact but the details of how the body got into the bog (had he been 'dropped' in?) and who it was remain conjecture.

Be that as it may, letters have arrived at the farm simply addressed to 'T'Drop', Haworth, probably because Joseph Heaton, John's brother, who had lived there, always put that address on the letters he sent out. (He was always referred to locally as 'Joseph o' t'Drop'.)

Little wonder that John knew his moors like the back of his hand, although he restricted his mole catching to the family property. Only occasionally was he tempted to cure the skins with salt and saltpetre: 'That's what they use for curing bacon, but four make a lovely pair of insoles for wellies in cold weather. They must need an awful lot to make a lady's fur coat,' he said, and also confirmed my worst fears that moles were on the increase, in our area at least.

There's more to catching a mole than simply putting down a trap. 'They're very "old-fashioned" – if you don't watch 'em, they go underneath the trap. You've got to get as cunning as they are and put down two traps, one behind the other. The mole thinks it's reight when it gets under one – then t'second one catches it. Sometimes we use a barrel and a jaw trap together.'

'A mole is a canny creature,' John told me. In wet weather the 'run' is likely to fill up with water, so he simply takes to the old stone drains, made long before pipes were thought of, until he comes to a wall, where he lodges, knowing the ground is likely to be drier there. In dry weather, too, he makes for the drains in search of any possible drinking water that might be about through seepage. A good mole catcher observes the weather and searches for his moles accordingly.

Working to rule was invented, apparently, by moles. They will die within twenty-four hours if they don't eat, and every two hours – on the hour – they will start their next work shift in search of worms or snails. Away go the strong front feet, digging and loosening the soil, with the snout working in perfect unison hoisting the stuff up on to the surface. Never was a creature more custom-built for its lifestyle. As every good dog knows, by the third hoist the mole is likely to be fairly near the surface and possibly vulnerable to a quick pounce.

'Are they really such a great nuisance?' I asked John. 'Oh, yes. In a meadow at hay time those hills'll blunt your blade in no time. And if it's for silage, a great big lump of soil in it can ruin it.' 'But don't they aerate the soil?' (I was temporarily on the side of the moles). 'In a way, but a mole just runs anywhere. With a machine you can "mole drain" a field in nice straight rows in no time at all.'

It appears to be thumbs down for the moles.

Some of John's moles found their way to the natural history section of the museum in Keighley, where they were dealt with by a taxidermist. One, taken about May time, was found to be heavily pregnant with seven young – apparently quite a record. Even the moles are healthy on Haworth moors!

John's face was a gentle russet smile surrounded by white hair. 'I remember a long time ago, when I was a lad, a man used to come round catching moles. If you gave him a shilling, he'd get rid of all your moles for you. If you didn't have any moles, you still gave him a shilling – otherwise you knew you'd have one pretty soon. I think he must have carried some in his pocket.'

How devious are the workings of moles – and men.

11

Old Timmy – Weaver and Legend
(or When Tilda Returned Timmy's Love Piece)

For centuries, the slopes of the Pennines vibrated to the noise of handloom weaving, an industry carried on by the hillfolk in their own cottages to provide them with the essentials of life. With the coming of the Industrial Revolution and the mills and power looms, the number of handloom weavers dwindled until finally they became a lost race.

Timmy Feather of Stanbury, who died in 1910, was the last of the handloom weavers in the area, but Martha Heaton remembered him vividly.

The time was August 1906, and ten-year-old Martha, her brother and her mother were visiting 'Old Timmy' at his cottage near Stanbury, overlooking the Haworth moors and Ponden Reservoir. It was the school holidays and they had walked with friends from Hawksbridge across Stanbury Heights and down the old Water Head Lane (now submerged beneath Sladen Reservoir) to Timmy's cottage at Buckley Green.

'Come on up t'cham'er an' aw'll weyve a pick or two for these lasses,' was Timmy's greeting. Not everyone received such a warm invitation 'up t'cham'er', for Timmy, having achieved something of a rarity value, sometimes resented the loss of his privacy. Local folk took their Sunday afternoon walks to try and catch a glimpse of him, and proud carriages bounced up the bumpy track to his cottage – Timmy had grown weary of being peered at through his window, even through the chinks in his curtains after he'd drawn them for his weekly 'wash down' on the Sabbath.

As it was, Martha and her family were admitted to the cottage only after Martha's mother had introduced herself through the closed door. 'Yah'd know my mother – she were Susey o' Owd Mick's at Bodkin Top.' Timmy was reassured. 'Ah knew Susey o' Owd Mick's. Come on in. Yah see, Ah get stalled o' foak comin' an' staring rahnd.'

Timmy was a little spare man, less than five feet tall, with white hair and beard, and like many who followed his noisy craft, he was very hard of hearing. His face was like the moors, weather-beaten, strong and full of spirit, and it bore witness to life as he had lived it. His staple food was porridge, for breakfast and supper, with havercake and cheese at midday, but once a week 'Wilsden Jack', the butcher, came with his cart, and then there was meat for dinner. Apparently Wilsden Jack had a sideline, too, for once he had offered to make Timmy's will for him, as Timmy could

Old Timmy Feather, handloom weaver and 'clog dancer of some renown'. He lived in a state of bachelor chaos. When he learned he was to receive an old age pension he was amazed. 'Well, Aw niver knew nowt like it', he remarked. 'They browt a looad o' coils afoor Cursmiss, an' now five shillin' i't week as long as aw live! An' aw've done nowt for nawther on 'em'.

neither read nor write. 'Nay, Ah've nowt to leave,' Timmy had said. 'Then Ah'll give thee summat,' was Wilsden Jack's reply.

Timmy's house was full of clocks, although few of them were actually going. Instead his day was ruled by the daylight – he got up at dawn and went to bed when it grew dark, and only during the dark winter days did he use an oil lamp for his weaving. Born on 20 January 1825, he was baptised on 25 July of that year by the Revd Patrick Brontë at Haworth. Being the last of his family to survive, he lived

Timmy, billycock and spinning wheel, with everything to hand, just where he could find it.

alone in his cottage in bachelor chaos, surrounded by storage tins of every description, basic cooking utensils and dishes, empty bird cages, sturdy old furniture, walls covered with pictures and a fine collection of old pottery arrayed on a delph rack. A spinning-wheel stood in pride of place by his armchair.

Following his invitation to his visitors, Timmy's old clogs clattered up the uneven steps to 't'cham'er' and Martha and her family followed him. In his younger days Timmy had been a clog dancer of some renown and, in spite of his small stature, he had once saved Stanbury from ignominy and shame in a jumping contest against Haworth. Now his clogs were purely for practical purposes, as was the ancient billycock that was his customary headgear.

The great handloom filled half the chamber, and deep notches on the sleyboard or 'hand tree' measured the imprint of the fingers and thumb of his left hand over a lifetime of weaving. The rest of the space was taken up with a bed, lumber and sacks of hen food for the poultry that seemed to be more at home in the house than out of it.

Timmy jumped on to the seat of the loom, began pedalling with his feet for the shaft of warp to come up and down, and then put a bobbin of spun cotton into the shuttle. With his hand he pulled the hand tree to and fro, the shuttle flying from one side to the other, and he was weaving the 'pick or two'.

Clogs pedalling, shuttle flying, gradually the piece materialised. Once Timmy had woven a special piece – to be taken by Lizzie Snowden, a neighbour's child, to Tilda who lived in the cottage at Buckleigh Farm. The piece of cotton had been a love offering but had been rejected by Tilda. 'Tak' it back – Ah doan't want it' – so Lizzie took the piece back and Timmy remained a bachelor. But Lizzie had carried other pieces for Timmy – to customers in Haworth and Oxenhope, walking over the moors on hot summer days with the heavy packs. Being only a little girl, on some of the hottest days the precious weaving had been rolled down the hills to take the weight off an aching back.

Each week Lizzie's mother made Timmy an apple pie and each day Lizzie's father sent Timmy a pint of milk from his smallholding at Buckley Green Bottom, for which Timmy paid one penny. Usually Lizzie took the milk, but one day her younger sister Lydia went along with it, shyly peeping through the doorway at Timmy. On seeing her his face had softened. 'Sithee Liddy, tak' this,' he said, taking a silver 3*d* piece out of a dirty linen bag. 'Ah 'ad a sister Liddy once.' And that was the last time Liddy took Timmy's milk. 'You'll tak' his milk no more,' said her mother, 'we ain't going to hev him paying 3*d* for a pint of milk.'

At last Timmy finished weaving the piece and detached it from the loom – two yards of very special cotton for which Martha's mother paid about three shillings. The following winter Martha wore an old woollen petticoat with a brand new cotton top and her father slept in a new cotton nightcap.

After thanking Timmy, goodbyes were said and the visitors left to make their way to Buckley Green Bottom, for Lizzie and Lydia's family were distant relatives of Martha's. Outside the smallholding Lizzie's mother had set up a sweet stall to attract the visitors who came to Timmy's cottage, and inside a kettle steamed on the hob, with its promise of a cup of tea. Next to the kettle a pan boiled away merrily – but its contents were difficult to distinguish. 'Ah'm boiling old Tim's cotton shirt – it 'ad gotten a reet bad colour,' was Lizzie's mother's matter-of-fact explanation.

Timmy Feather's funeral cortège at Buckley Green, 1910.

The view from Timmy Feather's cottage at Buckley Green, looking over to Ponden Reservoir with Rush Isles Farm at its near corner. The water tower for Watersheddles Reservoir, just in Lancashire but providing water for Yorkshire, can be seen on the skyline. Timmy would have seen both these reservoirs being built, changing his valley for ever.

Today Timmy's cottage has been absorbed into the cottage next door and his loom has long since gone. He is buried in old Haworth churchyard, alongside the path that leads to Sowden, one-time home of William Grimshaw. But the view from Buckley Green is very much as Timmy knew it. Ponden Reservoir, which Timmy would have seen being built, reflects the changing sky and on the horizon, in Lancashire, is the water tower of Watersheddles Reservoir, cradle of the River Worth. The wide sweep of the valley, the bracken and heather and moorland sheep, are still part of the world of Timmy Feather.

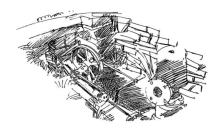

12

Quarries and Violins

The Stone heaves itself out of the surrounding moorland like some defiant relic of Druid ceremonies, gaunt and darkly lichen-covered against the sombre sweep of the Pennines. People who don't know call it 'The Gravestone', and that is the surprising size of it, but its origins are much more congenial. Amazing though it might seem, this miniature monolith is in fact the hearthstone of a blacksmith's shop, and a search among the surrounding heather reveals the actual foundations of the smithy. It is easy to imagine the leaping flames, and the hammer clanging on searing tools and horseshoes as the wind blows across the Brontë moors. The smithy was once a small but important part of West End Quarry which, along with Fieldhead and Crow Hill (all owned by the Barretts who at one time were said to be the biggest quarry owners in Yorkshire) devoured a section of what is now called Penistone Hill. Further over towards Marsh, Dimples and Bankfield Quarries (owned by Jaggers) chewed into the other side of the hill.

Today Penistone Hill has been tamed for tourists, with picnic areas and nature trails and probably the most expensive and impressive toilets in the Bradford Metropolitan Area. The quarries lie silent now – some have disappeared altogether, along with interesting traces of old coal workings, swept away under the expensive ministrations of countryside do-gooders. Others have become yet another car park.

But when I walked over Penistone Hill with Bill Packer, who had worked in the quarries there in the 1920s, battling against a biting November wind that was bringing tears to our eyes, Bill talked about 'my country'.

'This was where t'blacksmith stood, and t'bellows would be over there – we used to come in through a doorway here,' he said, pacing it out with a far-away look in his eye. 'My, it brings it all back. It was built with stone from t'Quarry, random stone same as these drystone walls round t'field.' Strange that these walls, a feature of the area, with their 'footings' of large boulders, fillings, 'throughs' to bind it all together, capstones and cripple holes, should outlast not only the men who made them so skilfully but also the quarries where they originated.

'It's bin a hard life when I come to look back,' said Bill, without a tinge of regret. 'You can't work stone in frosty weather – or snow – or rain – and we didn't get paid if we didn't work. In winter we sometimes went snow-shovelling for t'Corporation, but one time it were so bad and they needed that many that we didn't get a job

A scene typical of the stone quarries in and around Haworth in the early 1900s.

unless we took our own shovel. We got no holiday pay either – we took one week main holiday a year and we had to stand it ourselves.'

Explosives weren't used in Bill's day – they would have shattered the layers of comparatively soft sandstone – and all work was done by hand apart from the steam cranes. 'We fitted a big hook under the layer and the cranes came and pulled it out. We were "delvers" and were day-long hard at it dressing stone. You've got to get twenty foot down to get good stuff – first of all you had to "take a bearing", which meant getting rid of the "rag" or rubbish near the surface.'

There was also plenty to laugh at in the quarries. Jim Knowles was a delver – he was also renowned for being 'tight'. 'He never bought a newspaper, but every night he used to walk from Stanbury where he lived at that time to Haworth to read the ones in the Village Institute. We used to wonder what he put behind his toilet door, and then somebody said they'd been in and it was a sprig of heather! One night they were re-covering the billiard table at the Institute and he begged the old baize – he said it would make nice ties. Jim wouldn't waste food either. One of the delvers used to bring his Alsatian to work with him – it used to sleep in the cabin – and he slipped some dog biscuits into Jim's jock box. Come lunch time and Jim sat and ate 'em all – he said if his wife had put 'em up for 'im, he was going to eat 'em. Once somebody emptied Jim's jock box, fastened it to t'bench with a six-inch nail, then put the food back in. Jim were fair surprised when he tried to lift it.'

A Stanbury building contractor, Henry Metcalfe, was known at the quarries as 'Knock-on' Metcalfe. 'He was always coming to see how we were doing, then he'd say "Knock on, lads, you've done very well today, but do better tomorrow".'

Bill was often consulted about 'finds' on Penistone Hill, and when an old water pump, installed in about 1870, was uncovered, Bill remembered it in use at West End Quarry. It was worked by a windmill which stood on the hill top. A series of cogs, wheels and hawsers operated a 'push and pull' motion which pumped water from a natural spring up the hillside and over the top to a large tank at the quarry. In November 1926 there was a serious accident at West End Quarry. A man was up a ladder doing maintenance work on the windmill when his clothing caught in the sails and he choked to death. Shortly afterwards the windmill was dismantled when springs were discovered in the quarry, and the pump was presumably forgotten.

As well as being used on nearby Sladen Reservoir, stone from Penistone Hill travelled all over England, from Enfield in Middlesex to Morecambe, where it became part of the railway station and old pier. Heavy horse-drawn stone carts, with a brake on each wheel, trundled it across the moors and to Oxenhope Station, where it started its journey on the Worth Valley Railway.

Another regular traveller on the railway was Kershaw Barrett, owner of West End, Crow Hill and Fieldhead Quarries. Every Thursday he visited the Stone Exchange in Sunbridge Road, Bradford. 'He was always at the last minute,' remembered his daughter Sarah, who lived in Stanbury. 'He used to run down Moorhouse Lane and leap over the wall to cut a corner off. If he was late the train would wait for him to arrive, and he always combined a visit to the Stone Exchange with a trip round the Bradford antique shops. I remember he once bought some beautiful imitation birds under a glass case and they flew about and drank water.'

Kershaw combined quarrying with music, and Sunday nights at home were always musical evenings. Although he never had a music lesson in his life and could play but little, he was a violin-maker of wide renown, and his workroom was in the former schoolroom of old Haworth Free Grammar School, Marshlands, where he lived.

Kershaw Barrett, quarry owner and violin maker, in his workshop at Marshlands where he lived. This was originally Haworth Free Grammar School. (Reproduced courtesy of Robert Sunderland)

'He was more interested in his violins than in his quarries, and, after varnishing them, used to hang them out to dry on a cherry tree in the garden in good weather. He believed the best violins were made in sunny places.' Once, Albert Sandler came to play at the old Keighley Hippodrome, which alas is no more, and Kershaw took one of his violins for him to use. Away from the quarries, Kershaw was normally 'happy to be in his own home with his violins' – except on Sundays. Then the family walked two miles and back to Haworth Baptist Church three times, unless they were lucky enough to be invited to a meal in Haworth. Sarah showed me a photograph of Kershaw's Sunday School class of twenty-five boys, most of whom were killed in the First World War.

The quarries were opened by Kershaw's father, Charles, who himself once constructed a grand piano, and Sarah had a letter from him to Kershaw, dated July 1882, written when Kershaw was away from home on quarry business. The spelling is bizarre, the writing beautifully formed: 'Mr John Wilkinson sent an order for ten trucks of Walstones Pitched we should like to know something moore about the Man if he his sound if you could make some inquiry privately it would be very well.' Grandpa Charles was obviously a cautious man, although a man of faith. 'I ever remain your Dear Parant in the one Hope, Charles Barrett.' Grandma adds a loving postscript: 'You have pased firs clas in Building Construction their will be a prize for you.'

Tom Stell's seat at the edge of the quarries on the Oxenhope Road.

Another letter to Kershaw, dated December 1903, from a 'cattle spice' supplier, leaves much to ponder on – 'hoping you are all well boath temperal & Spiretual, mentely & physical. And may God Bless you boath in time & internety there his only a step between us & death from yours truly. . . .' It is to be hoped that the man got his order in time!

Kershaw was a man of wit and learning, and when the local paper referred to him as 'the late Kershaw Barrett' in an article about his 'famous fiddles', he sent a caustic letter to them quoting Mark Twain who, similarly dealt with by the American Associated Press, had said 'The report of my death was an exaggeration'.

By the side of the road that goes over the moors from Stanbury to Oxenhope, at the top of the rise by Grove Hill Dyke and within a stone's throw of the old quarries, stands 'Tom Stell's seat', a memorial dated 1932 to a local man 'who loved these moors'. It was hewn from a single block of stone from Crow Hill Quarry and taken to its magnificent vantage point on a flat cart by three quarrymen – a feat of love and strength. Memorial to Tom Stell it might be, but it is also a tribute to the men of Penistone Hill Quarries – to their forthrightness, humour and hard work.

13

Rahnd an' Rahnd with Arthur

'Me mother wer allus a creeaking gate. Me father browt us all up, an' he were a careful man. He had to be, being a small farmer. An' he deed as he lived – careful. On t'day he deed he'd been dahn to t'hens to collect t'eggs. There weren't mony 'cos t'hens were off lay an' he were ban to sell 'em t'day after. An' as he came to t'barn door he had to lift it 'cos it were ill-fitting. That's what did it. He dropped dahn deead on t'spot. And dost know, he didn't break an egg, nor his watch norther. 'E were careful to t'end. An' t'next day they came to collect t'hens and offered us six shillings apiece for 'em. Wi' me father ligging deead in t'house we knew they'd offered 'im eight shillings just afore he deed.'

Arthur Smith lives at Lower Marsh, Oxenhope, in two cottages rolled into one. The result is a confusion of doors, and much-lived-in rooms where most of the chairs are already occupied by stuffed toy animals made by his late wife Wynn to support the funds of a local band. On the walls are photographs of badgers, for Arthur's son, Philip, is a keen badger-watcher. From the back of his home Arthur looks out over the Worth Valley Railway line to Oxenhope in its green bowl of hills, a maze of millstone grit houses punctuated by mill chimneys. From the front, looking to Higher Marsh across the fields, stands Hanging Gate Farm, where Arthur was brought up and where he lived for thirty years.

I first met Arthur Smith when he came to sweep my chimney. He clattered into the kitchen with his rods like a conflagrated Marley's ghost. 'Wheere is it?', he demanded, getting down to business straight away. 'It's in the sitting-room; it's a bad one. We've just had the fireplace put back and it hasn't been used for years. I think there's a midfeather down or something.' I was trying to sound knowledgeable. 'I'll soon show it who's t'maister,' he threatened. And he did, although at one point he nearly gave in. 'It's not going to go,' he panted, some of his confidence gone. 'Rubbish. Just give it another push,' I persuaded. Sure enough it went, and thankfully I put the kettle on for a cup of tea.

As Arthur supped he chatted, and as he chatted he smoked, knocking his cigarette ash into his sooty cloth cap and spurning the ashtray provided. He told me tales of his boyhood at Hanging Gate Farm, and always his father, who'd won the Military Medal in the First World War for gallantry, figured prominently.

Arthur Smith in the garden of his cottage at Lower Marsh. Five minutes' walk away is Hanging Gate Farm where he grew up.

Haytime at Hanging Gate always started on Arthur's birthday, 17 June, 'an' it were an exciting time for us kids'. The wooden hayrakes were put to swell in the water-butts to prevent the teeth dropping out, and the mowing machine – on hire from t'Free Schooil Farm down the road – would arrive drawn by two horses, Paddy and Duke. The first day was a lark, with the machine doing all the work, but after that the real business started. 'Rahnd an' rahnd an' rahnd we went – tossing it and turning it for t'wind to blow through reet nicely. Hay took some makin' in them days.' It was raked into turnings, then ricklings, then tossed again, and there was no slacking for Arthur and his brother. They had to keep up with the men, 'otherwise Uncle George used to be tapping us 'eels with his rake'. Finally it was ready for 'leeading' (this was before the days of balers), by which time it was prickly stuff, and the result was sore arms. It was tossed into the barn loose, shaken out, then it was 'rahnd an' rahnd an' rahnd again, treading it down so that in winter it could be cut with a long hay knife for "fothering". Any hay not properly trod used to "bounce abaht" when cut, and any that was below par would be put aside as "bull hay"' – only the best was good enough for the precious milk cattle.

Life at Hanging Gate wasn't easy, especially in the early days. Arthur's father's first purchase was two Irish heifers from Skipton market for about £9 each, but one died within a week. Soon afterwards he bought 350 Irish pullets, 'all Irish', who were joined every morning at feeding time by some peacocks who lived nearby, but they, too, started dying and his father had to take barrowloads of dead hens to the Old Oxenhope Mill boiler house to get rid of them.

Gradually the farm pulled itself up by its bootstrings, 'but we allus had plenty to eat – milk and eggs and butter, sad cakes and suet cakes, and in winter time, wi' big fat legs and short breeches, we were reight sore. T'first thing you smelt when you went into Oxenhope classroom was Fullers Earth Cream. We were allus doing summat, laiking didn't come into it, haymaking, muckspreading, drystone-walling, egg collecting, an' of course milking. In haymaking time we'd finish in t'fields at eleven o'clock at neet and then start milking, ready to tak' it i' great churns to Oxenhope Station first thing next morning. Sometimes we'd go on to John Willie Ratcliffe's joiner's shop and help him boil pitch for his coffins – we were allus throng as Throp's wife.'

Arthur's father was also careful with his candles. In wintertime he'd cut a candle into two unequal pieces and milk eleven cows in the mistle with the larger piece and four cows in the stable with the smaller piece. He'd got it timed to a fine art and the candle power just held out if he worked fast – and all by hand. Although the farmhouse had gas, 'we were at the end of the line and it'd burn alreet for half an hour an' then go out. We used to leeave it for a bit until we smelt gas and then we'd leet it again.' With another small piece of candle the cows were 'fothered', sawdusted down, and the milk cooled. 'That was what you might call motoring.'

The milk separator used to fascinate Arthur. Milk was poured in at the top, you turned a handle, there was a whining noise and the separated milk for the pigs came out of one spout at the bottom and the cream out of another spout. How it happened he could never figure. Tuesday was butter-making day for Arthur's father.

'He used to churn all day and he had a big butter worker an' all.' As soon as the butter 'broke' in the churn it was put on the butter worker, salt was added, and then it was rolled until it was bone dry. Then it was chopped off with butter pats into pieces ranging from 2 oz to 2 lb, wrapped in greaseproof paper and put in the butter basket ready for delivery, on foot, on Wednesday. Arthur's father milked by hand until the last five years of his life, when he chopped the end of his thumb off in the turnip machine. 'It were all finger and thumb milking with the little Irish heifers, and they couldn't half rattle it art.' Eventually milk and butter were collected by a dairy. 'It were a godsend for t'little farmers. Bert used to come and collect it and he'd come in and hev his breakfast – good home-fed bacon with thick yellow fat. Then he'd have an hour on t'piano – he were a club pianist – and he used to rattle away for a good hour, then go on his way rejoicing. That's why they've put "t'Spy in the Cab" – there were too much mucking abaht.'

When Arthur left school at fourteen 'it were awther t'black shop or t'mill', so he went to work at Old Oxenhope Mill, starting at ten minutes to six every morning 'to get things ready for t'lassies coming at 6 o'clock', and finishing at 6 o'clock at night. One early job was to get the gaslights lit, and last thing at night they had to be turned off. This was done in the toilet on the third floor, and Arthur could just time it so that he could turn off the gas, belt down the three storeys and be by the outside door by the time the last lamp faded. Old Oxenhope Mill was steam

Old Oxenhope Mill and row of cottages, all burned down in 1962. Arthur Smith's working hours, aged fourteen, were from 5.50 a.m. to 6.00 p.m.

powered and the machinery was old. Sometimes if the crank on the engine wasn't left at the top at night, the lads had to move it manually the following morning, heaving with a heavy bar, to get the mill going for the day. 'It could take us half an hour, and that was before we really started working.'

In the packing sheds, which were always warm from the great flue, hung rows of big bags for wool waste. Another job for Arthur and his pals was to get inside these bags of waste and again it was a question of 'rahnd an' rahnd an' rahnd', jumping up and down to press down the waste before 'Willie o't' Free Schooil' came to collect it and take it to Oxenhope Station.

Old Oxenhope Mill had an interesting sideline besides textiles – goldfish. The hot water from the boiler fed into two small tanks and the thrifty millowners used to breed goldfish in these, selling them at 3*d* for a little one, a tanner for a big one. A slightly less profitable enterprise was the trout in the main mill dam – somehow or other these always disappeared during the night.

Today Old Oxenhope Mill is no more. It was burned down in 1962, when its timbers, soaked with oil from the wool, were rich fuel for the flames. Gone is the solid mahogany office furniture, the row of cottages kept warm by the mill flue, the towering chimney. Only the mill dam remains, and memories in the minds of local folk like Arthur Smith.

Even Hanging Gate Farm is altered now, 'modernised' to suit the times, no longer even a farm. But as Arthur looks across at it from his cottage at Marsh, it symbolises his boyhood, where he first learned the value of hard work, in retrospect at least.

'I'd an Uncle Milton who sold eggs. He was a butcher in Bradford, and he allus charged t'same for t'big uns and t'little uns. He said there was a day's work in awther,' recalls Arthur.

14

Portrait of Patrick

'My Dear Saucy Pat . . .' wrote a young woman, very much in love, to her husband-to-be six weeks before their wedding day. Nothing very unusual about that – except that the year was 1812 and the bridegroom in question was Patrick Brontë, later to become that much-maligned parson of St Michael and All Angels' Church, Haworth. In those days young ladies were expected to be prim right up to their wedding day and beyond, but in the letter that followed Maria Branwell declares her love clearly, teases young Patrick soundly – and informs him that most of her worldly goods have been lost in a shipwreck en route from Penzance to Woodhouse Grove School near Leeds. Maria had been staying at the school as the guest of her Aunt and Uncle Fennell (her uncle was the school's first headmaster), and it was here that she'd been swept off her feet in a whirlwind romance when the new school examiner, Patrick Brontë, made his appearance. All this is unlike the usual picture painted of Patrick and Maria – posterity often perverts the truth for drama's sake, and the image of a stern, aloof, grief-ridden father is good for Brontë business.

Patrick Brunty was born in humble circumstances in Ireland on St Patrick's Day, 17 March 1777, the first of ten children. His mother was originally Roman Catholic, his father Protestant, which could account for his independence of spirit (some might call it stubbornness), and the Wesleyan movement not only influenced his early manhood but also helped to pay for his university education (Maria's family were also Wesleyans).

When Patrick left school he went to work as a blacksmith's assistant, then as a linen weaver, but one day the Revd Andrew Harshaw noticed his love of books and opened his own library to him, and from then on Patrick studied to become a teacher, working often by rushlight after his day at the weaving loom (a fact that could account for his exceedingly bad eyesight in later years). Eventually Mr Harshaw procured him a teaching post at Glascar Presbyterian Church School, after which he went to a larger parish church school at Drumballerony, where he also taught the children of the Rector, the Revd Thomas Tighe. A friend of the Wesleys, Thomas Tighe was a staunch supporter of the Wesleyan influence within the Established Church, and soon recognised Patrick's potential, both as a scholar and also possibly as a man of God. He therefore started to tutor Patrick, hoping that eventually he would

Patrick Brontë, Curate-in-Charge of Haworth Church from 1820 to 1861.

go to Cambridge, where he himself had been a student and where the Wesleyan influence was strong, and also that he would enter the ministry. Fortunately this idea of the ministry was also forming in Patrick's mind. At that time there was no entrance examination to Cambridge, just personal recommendation and, with Mr Tighe's backing and financial help from the Wesleyans, Patrick entered the University as a 'sizar', a kind of servant to one of the Fellows, thus getting his instruction at a cut-price rate.

When Patrick came to St John's College on 1 October 1802, the porter wrote 'Patrick Branty' in the register, but two days later when the man made the same entry for Patrick's first day of residence, Patrick crossed it out and deliberately wrote, for the first time, 'Patrick Brontë'. (Three years earlier Lord Nelson, one of his heroes, had been created Duke of Brontë.)

Patrick was determined to succeed, and took pride in his achievements. Two books with beautiful leather-tooled bindings – Homer's *Iliad* in Greek and Latin, and a rare edition of the *Odes and Letters* of Horace – carry Patrick's eloquent inscription: 'My Prize Book for having always kept in the first class at St. John's College, Cambridge. P. Brontë A.B. To be retained semper.' Intimations of immortality, perhaps? Similarly, years later, Charlotte sent a selection of her poetry to Robert Southey in Keswick, asking whether she should become a poet. Although the answer was a definite 'No', she wrote on the cover 'Southey's advice, to be kept for ever'.

Patrick loved books but believed that they were for using, and scribbled copious and revealing notes in many of his. The Cambridge Horace is covered both with his own and Branwell's writing, legacy from the hours the two of them pored over it together as Patrick taught his son. Branwell must have enjoyed his studies, because while working at Broughton-in-Furness aged twenty-three he translated the first book of *Odes* just for pleasure, and years after his death, when it was published privately, the poet John Drinkwater said it contained 'passages of clear lyrical beauty'. Poor Branwell, potential genius but unstable. His father patiently reinstated him after each fall, but one step lower down the ladder, until finally there was nowhere left for him to go. And yet he loved his son, in whom he had so many hopes, and nursed him tenderly in his last illness. Afterwards, Charlotte likened their relationship to that of David and Absolom.

Ironic that the young curate, Willie Weightman, brilliant classical scholar and irrepressible companion of the parsonage daughters (they christened him 'Celia Amelia') possessed every attribute that Patrick could have wanted in a son, but also died young, from cholera, after visiting a stricken Haworth household. 'We were always like father and son,' said Patrick, preaching at Weightman's funeral one of his rare sermons from notes (he normally preached extempore, but the Weightman funeral sermon was to be published later).

Another well-used, well-scribbled-in book is Patrick's *Modern Domestic Medicine* by Thomas John Graham. Patrick was a fighter, and fought the disease surrounding him at home and in Haworth as well as he could, but they were primitive times, as shown by Patrick's notes under 'Anaesthetics and Operations' – 'Care must be taken not to bring the flame of a candle near the operator, otherwise there might be a destructive explosion.' Sobering thought. Results of Patrick's talks with medical friends were also recorded. Toothache must have been a less serious blight at Haworth, and from Patrick's do-it-yourself dentistry notes we learn that charcoal powder was one of the best dentifrices and 'oak makes the best charcoal'. He suffered from dyspepsia, attributed to his mother's bread-making, and his favourite cure, written in the book, must have packed quite a punch. It consisted of Epsom salts, tincture of red lavender, cascarilla, vitriolic acid and hot water. 'Take when necessary, one wine glass after dinner.' And yet he lived to a ripe old age!

Patrick's first appointment after Cambridge was as curate at Wethersfield in Essex, where he fell in love with Mary Burder, a reputed beauty. Her guardian, however, would not hear of a match with a penniless Irish curate, and the affair ended with heartbreak on both sides. From Wethersfield, Patrick went to Wellington in Shropshire, where he met William Morgan who was to become a lifelong friend, and then to Dewsbury, his first Yorkshire home. While at Dewsbury he started writing poetry again, and then came another move to Hartshead where, for the first time, he was perpetual curate of his own parish. These were troublesome times in Yorkshire, with the Luddites attacking mills where the installation of new machinery threatened their jobs, and Rawfolds Mill at Liversedge, near Cleckheaton, became a well-known victim of their violence. Patrick's habit of having a pistol always handy stemmed from his Hartshead days when, although partly in sympathy with the Luddite cause (they were, after all, at starvation level), he would not countenance law-breaking, and therefore became a marked man. It was also while he was at Hartshead that Patrick met and fell in love with Maria Branwell, and the couple were married at a double wedding ceremony at Guiseley Church on 29 December 1812; the other couple being married were William Morgan and Jane Fennell, Maria's cousin. Each of the bridegrooms officiated at the marriage of the other, and each of the brides was bridesmaid for the other.

Patrick and his bride were wonderfully happy; his writing seemed to be flourishing with his 'Cottage Poems' being the best-known, and first Maria and then Elizabeth were born, before the Brontës' next move to Thornton in 1815 – with Haworth only seven miles away directly across the moors.

Charlotte Brontë was born in Thornton in April 1816, and just over a year later came Branwell, the son Patrick had been hoping for. In 1818 Emily was born, and eighteen months later Anne – the Brontë family was complete and ready for its final move to Haworth on 20 April 1820.

It was not long before the first blow fell. Maria died of cancer a little after a year in Haworth, and Patrick was left with six small children to look after. He decided he

Church Street in Haworth leading past the church to the Brontë Parsonage Museum. The taller gable-end on the right of the Parsonage was added by John Wade, Patrick Brontë's successor. The school and Sunday School built by Patrick Brontë are on the right of the picture.

must find them a mother, and his first choice was Elizabeth Firth of Thornton. When she turned him down he thought of Mary Burder again, but by this time she, too, was not interested. There was nothing else for it; Aunt Branwell, Maria's sister, who had come to Haworth during Maria's illness, must remain in Haworth, which she didn't like, to look after the children.

Even after Maria's death life at the parsonage was neither dull nor narrow. Patrick was an enlightened man of great enthusiasms and his advice, when given, was sometimes surprising. The wife of a local cleric came to him in distress because of her husband's unholy behaviour. 'Leave him for ever and go home, if you have a home to go to,' said Patrick, ahead of his time.

Patrick was very conscious of the poor living conditions of his parishioners and, with local government almost non-existent, he and a committee were responsible for whitewashing and cleaning houses during a cholera epidemic, numbering houses for easier identification, supplying clothes and bedding to the needy, keeping the roads as clear as possible – and erecting a lock-up prison. The arrival in Haworth in 1850 of a government health inspector was the result of a petition he instigated. He also campaigned for piped water and efficient drainage for the village, and used his not inconsiderable knowledge of the law to help his parishioners. He was involved in social reform, and *The Times* quoted his denunciation of the new Poor Law Act which he felt did nothing to help the needy. A letter dated 1854, and later acknowledged as being in Charlotte's handwriting, was written on behalf of Patrick to convene a meeting in Haworth to raise funds for widows and orphans of the Crimean War. It was Patrick who set the ball rolling for Haworth to be separated from Bradford parish; he built the Sunday School, still in use, installed the first organ and the peal of six bells, and was instrumental in having churches built at Stanbury and Oxenhope.

People point at the bullet holes in Haworth Church tower and say he was mad. Not so. The pistol he kept near him from his Luddite days, purely for safety's sake, had to be discharged each day; what better place to fire it than over the graveyard where he was least likely to kill someone? He was a good shot and enjoyed grouse shooting with Willie Weightman, but Emily, although he taught her to shoot, would never join them. Her feelings were that if they had to shoot at something, why couldn't they leave the birds alone and shoot each other! A letter to Sir John Murray, Master General of Ordnance, shows Patrick's interest in guns to be quite technical – he suggested improvements to the construction of muskets which, however, were not adopted.

Patrick enjoyed his children, discussing with them the goings-on in the world outside Haworth, arranging drawing and music lessons, walking on the moors and often accompanying them on their travels, and they certainly travelled more than most Victorian young people. After taking Charlotte and Emily to Brussels – they stayed in London en route, at the famous Chapter Coffee House for a few nights so that Patrick could show them around – it's thought that Patrick realised one of his own dreams and visited the scene of the Battle of Waterloo.

All this, and much more, hardly points to a hard and bitter man, living within himself. Blow after blow had fallen, his children had all died prematurely and he was almost blind, yet he accepted it all, trusting in his Lord – he never despaired and became broken.

To read his letters and the notes scribbled in his books, to stand in his study and look through the window to the old church tower, is to feel the deep sadness of this man, but also to appreciate his great humanity and courage, his initial zest for living, and the battles he fought and won. He was not only father of genius; he also stands well in his own right – as Patrick Brontë.

15

Wycoller

Wycoller is a dream of a village clustered beside its beck and bridges but, reminiscent of Brig o'Doon, it disappeared as a living community for about a hundred years, and only began to materialise again in about 1973. Its history goes back to Anglo-Saxon times, when settlers from nearby Trawden decided to farm in the lovely valley; the name means 'dairy farm among the alders', and although the alders have now gone, the land around Wycoller continues to be good for cattle.

In the fourteenth century the De Lacy family of Clitheroe Castle established two cattle-rearing stations there, enclosing them with the curious vaccary walls – large upright slabs of heavy stone, which are still a feature of Wycoller and give it an almost prehistoric atmosphere.

In the seventeenth and eighteenth centuries Wycoller was a busy little community of yeoman farmers and handloom weavers, and a T-junction was made off the main Pennine pack-horse route between Clitheroe and Pontefract which passed close by, so that it came down to Wycoller and the weaving was collected. Some of the old paving stones on the route are still there just beneath the grass and can easily be uncovered.

Two old bridges cross the beck in the centre of Wycoller, close by the ford; 'Sallie's Bridge' is a 700-year-old double-arched packhorse bridge, and a deep groove worn along it bears witness to the clogs of the handloom weavers as they clattered over it with their heavy packages. Close by is a much older, more primitive clapper bridge – simply heavy stone slabs supported on uprights – and this, too, had a deep groove worn by countless clogs, until many years ago a farmer's sister fell off it into the beck (which must have been in full spate) and she died as a result – after that the farmer came along and chiselled it flat. Two or three hundred yards up the beck is the most primitive bridge of all – an ancient clam bridge, which is merely a huge slab supported on opposite banks of the river. This takes Wycoller back to prehistory, and people have certainly been around in the area for quite some time, as many flint arrowheads have been found and there is a Bronze Age burial mound on the moors.

Wycoller Hall is the home of legend, and its ruins by the beck are compelling and mysterious. It originated in the mid-sixteenth century as a fairly humble farmstead,

Wycoller. In the background is Sallie's Bridge, an ancient double-arched packhorse bridge. In the foreground is an older and more primitive clapper bridge.

but as it was the home of the Hartley family who were living in Wycoller at least from 1416, there could have been a building on the site even earlier than that.

In August 1611 Elizabeth Hartley married Nicholas Cunliffe, and for the next 200 years there were Cunliffes at Wycoller Hall. Gradually they improved and extended it, but it was not until a year after Henry Owen Cunliffe arrived on the scene in 1773 that it fully blossomed. Henry Owen was the great-nephew of Henry Cunliffe of Wycoller, and when Uncle Henry died in 1773 he left the Hall and estates to Henry Owen on condition that he would assume the surname of Cunliffe, which he did. Henry Owen Cunliffe was a short, pompous little man who fancied himself very much as a country gentleman, so much so that he was nicknamed 'Squire' Cunliffe and even on occasion 'The Baron'. On arriving at Wycoller he felt that it was slightly inferior to the homes of the neighbouring gentry, and promptly set about a scheme of improvement and enlargement that

Wycoller, the clapper bridge showing the groove made by clogged feet over the centuries. In the background is all that remains of old Wycoller Hall. Dating back to the mid-sixteenth century, and possibly before, it is a legend in itself.

resulted in Wycoller Hall as it was in its heyday – but also left him mortgaged up to the ears for the rest of his life.

During the alterations Henry took himself off to live at the Red Lion at Colne (there was never a public house at Wycoller), but kept popping over from time to time to keep an eye on his Hall. A porch topped with carved finials was added to the front of the house, and also a row of fine mullioned windows. A mock-Tudor fireplace now graced one end of the main room, with carved shields at either side bearing the Cunliffe crest and a stone bench curving inside the huge hearth. At the right-hand side is a curious keyhole-shaped recess which has been given many explanations, the most likely being that it was simply used for drying timber. The mullioned windows and fireplace have weathered the passage of time and can still be seen today. New windows were fitted elsewhere in the house, part of which by this time was three-storeyed, the whole was generally improved, and the farmhouse surroundings gave way to pleasant gardens, complete with fish-pond. When the improvements were finished, Henry came back to the Hall, bringing with him a bride.

Just beyond the fish-pond, which is still there, is the old cock-fighting pit, but you have to know exactly where to look for it as it is now just another dip in the field. Tethering rings and cockspurs have been found there and Henry Owen was a keen follower of this so-called sport. Indeed, there is a story that even on his deathbed he would have a cock fight, so the cocks were brought into his bedroom and mirrors arranged so that he could watch even though his movements were limited.

His large mortgages apparently made no difference to 'The Baron's' lifestyle; entertainment at the Hall was lavish, especially at Christmas, and it is easy to imagine a fire burning in the huge fireplace, wine flowing, and Henry Owen presiding over a banquet with his guests. He was also keen on hunting and shooting, with its accompanying round of hospitality, and one of the many ghost stories attached to the Hall and village owes its origin to this.

Apparently one of the hunts was a complete disaster, with never a fox in sight until it was time to return home. Suddenly a fox broke cover and ran towards Wycoller, with Henry and the hounds in full pursuit. In at the front door of the Hall it ran, up the main staircase and into my lady's bedroom, still pursued by Henry on his horse and the hounds. This naturally came as something of a shock to the lady, who happened to be in bed at the time, and she expired on the spot. Now there are tales of a phantom horseman and a lady in black who haunt Wycoller, and the lady in particular has made appearances in fairly recent times. There are one or two variations on this theme, but they all have two things in common – the phantom horseman and the lady in black.

Near to the ruins of Wycoller Hall stands a huge aisled barn which was erected in 1630. The timbers are magnificent and some of them could have been second-hand when they were put into the barn. The roof and rafters are supported by great oak pillars which stand on stone bases to protect the wood from rotting, and in these pillars can be seen the holes which were used as they were heaved into position. One of these pillars also has a strange mark on it – some say it is a mason's mark, but a more interesting theory has been put forward that it is the remains of an old game of 'Nine Men's Morris' played by the men who erected the barn.

In about 1774 the barn also became a coach-house, and two arched doorways were made and cobbles laid on part of the earth floor. A coach road wound up behind the village, bounded at some points by the vaccary walling, and two rather grand stone gateposts can still be seen by the side of the Haworth road as it drops into Laneshaw Bridge.

Henry Owen Cunliffe died in 1818 and the Hall stood empty after that. Strangely, life in the village was then at its peak, and in 1821 there were 350 people registered as living at Wycoller. The Hall gradually became a ruin, its demise hastened by the fact that stone from it was carried off by thrifty folk to repair or build anew, and its grand entrance porch was re-erected en bloc against a building in Trawden, complete with fancy finials. As the Hall declined, so did the village. The industrial age was upon us, and the mills in Lancashire could offer a better living than the handlooms in Wycoller. Soon there was nobody left and the cottages, most of them built in about 1600, also began to fall down and even disappear altogether. The village slept – only on the surrounding farms were cattle reared, as from ancient times.

If Charlotte Brontë visited Wycoller, as is probable, it would have been at the start of this period of decay. Certainly the Hall would have been empty, but it must have retained enough of its appeal for her to take it to her heart. It is thought to be the 'Ferndean Manor' of *Jane Eyre*, the place of peace where Rochester and Jane were finally united, and indeed its sad decline might have added to her imagination as the two were finally brought together after all their trials.

Another link with *Jane Eyre* – and another Wycoller ghost. There is a certain type of phantom that has a definite leaning towards the north of England. It is called a 'Guytrash', and takes the form of either a large dog or a riderless horse. There are tales of a Guytrash skulking in the lanes around Wycoller, and no doubt Charlotte knew them. Here she describes Jane Eyre's first meeting with Rochester:

'I heard a rush under the hedge, and close down by the hazel stems glided a great dog, whose black and white colour made him a distinct object against the trees. It was exactly one mask of Bessie's Gytrash [*sic*] – a lion-like creature with long hair and a huge head; it passed me, however, quietly enough. . . . The horse followed – a tall steed, and on its back a rider. The man, the human being, broke the spell at once. Nothing ever rode the Gytrash.' The rider, of course, was Rochester, who shortly afterwards sustained a nasty fall, and the dog was Pilot, but the picture conjured up for us is sinister – could it be that for a brief moment Charlotte was combining two of Wycoller's ghostly characters?

In 1896 Wycoller looked likely to disappear for ever as plans were put forward to build a reservoir in the Wycoller Valley, or Dene, just above the village, to supply the needs of the growing town of Colne. Although the embankment would have been built just above the village and none of the farms would have been submerged, it is probable that stone from the derelict village would have been used in the construction, and possibly the farms would have suffered the same fate as those on Haworth Moor – depopulation because of seepage. New roads would have been made through the quiet valley, and reservoir appendages would have been strewn over a wide area. Mercifully it was decided that the project would be too costly, and the possibility of underground water was explored instead. Eventually, water was discovered 420 feet below the surface, a bore-hole was established, and pumping operations began.

Now and then people came to live in Wycoller, but nobody really awakened the sleeper, and nobody stayed long, apart from Tom Emmott. He came at the end of the 1940s and lived in Wycoller Cottage, an ancient building with a lant trough in its garden and wuzzling holes in its outside walls, left behind by handloom weavers of long ago. He was an eccentric and a dissembler and eventually developed a strong persecution complex, writing letters to many prominent people, including the Archbishop of Canterbury. He wrote an autobiography, full of delusions, and a book called *Eamot Eternal*, which traced the Emmott family back through the ages to the lost continent of Atlantis, with always one Tom Emmott as the hero. In 1959 he formed the Lancastrian Party and stood as Member of Parliament in the general election – unfortunately he forfeited his deposit, but a carving on a stone in the garden of Wycoller Cottage left his party to posterity – it simply says 'LANCASTRIAN PARTY H.Q.'

During Tom Emmott's stay in Wycoller I visited the village one day, imagining it to be empty. To my surprise a figure hurled itself out of Wycoller Cottage and arranged a few books, then peered through a window to watch my reaction. I was so surprised that I didn't go near enough to look at them, unfortunately, otherwise I might have been the possessor of one of his books.

In 1950 the 'Friends of Wycoller' were formed to try and preserve to some extent the village and Hall. They cleared the Hall of unwelcome vegetation, laid flagstones in the main room and renovated the fireplace, but the task was too much for them and their limited finances and finally, in 1973, Lancaster County Council bought the estate and designated it a Country Park and Conservation Area. Cottages were renovated as people began to drift back into the village to live – Wycoller yawned and stretched itself.

Keith Houlker was Country Park Warden for Wycoller until 1984. He loves and understands Wycoller well, and it is his idea of heaven. Keith thought that Lancashire County Council was administrating Wycoller wisely, particularly in making the large car park well away from the village and in restoring the old aisled barn and coach-house, but he worried about pressure on the village from tourists who are inevitably attracted by their efforts. Each year their numbers increase. 'We had no option but to do what we did,' he said, referring to the restoration of the village, but he wondered where it would end.

The usual picnic tables have appeared where the Hall gardens once were, and arrows, blobs and notices are everywhere, very similar to some parts of the Brontë moors. There is also a danger that guest-houses might proliferate, or a large restaurant might open, and if this happened Keith and apparently everybody in the village felt it would be the end of Wycoller.

Louise Hartley, formerly Wilkinson, had an idyllic childhood roaming round the ruins of Wycoller with her brothers and sisters. 'We ran up and down the stairs and peeped out of the windows – we used to think it was great and that they would never be lived in again.' Louise was brought up at Lowlands Farm on the edge of Wycoller and for a time theirs was the only family around. Once, when the children were out sledging, a newspaper photographer saw them and took a picture. 'He must have thought "How quaint".' They appeared in three newspapers and finally television came to Wycoller and they featured in *Look North*. 'They had us doing silly things like running across bridges and waving.'

Louise moved from Wycoller when she married – to Laneshaw Bridge two miles away – but she came back every day while her father had the farm. When it was sold Louise and her husband bought the barn and turned it into a home for themselves and their two small children. She admitted to being a 'solitary' and looked back to the Wycoller of her childhood with nostalgia. 'I wish it could have stayed like that for ever!'

People do not seem to stay very long in Wycoller. Many come in full of enthusiasm for country life, then gradually it wanes and they move out again. Some move out for the opposite reason. They acquire a taste for country life but are frustrated when they are unable to buy land from Lancashire County Council to start a smallholding or something similar.

Today Wycoller is still a place of infinite charm nestling in its sheltered valley – smoke curls upwards from the chimneys of clustered grey stone houses, the beck meanders beneath its bridges as it has always done, and close by are the ruins of the old Hall; children splash happily by the ancient ford and there is a little café that was once a cowshed where a fire burns in a black kitchen grate and you can get toasted teacakes and pots of tea, not to mention homemade cakes. It has been run by the same family for twenty-two years.

Where there could so easily have been nothing but piles of stones and decay, there is life and the sound of people, but just underneath the surface there is still a slight feeling of uncertainty as Wycoller struggles to adjust itself after its long sleep.

16

Incumbents and Trustees

The official list of Haworth incumbents, to be found inside the church, begins in 1653, when the Revd J. Collier had the cure of souls in the village. These were troublesome times, with England split by civil war, and this unfortunate man was expelled from his pulpit in 1654, presumably for his Royalist tendencies. Two Puritan curates followed – E. Garforth, who lasted only one year, and Robert Town – but in 1662, with the monarchy restored, the faithful Collier was reinstated at Haworth.

The story of Haworth Church, however, goes back long before 1653, although its very early history can only be conjecture. What is certain, however, is that in 1317 the vicar of Bradford and the people of Haworth were ordered to pay a stipend to the curate of Haworth, based on those due 'from ancient times'. Obviously a church existed in Haworth at least as far back as the thirteenth century.

In 1338 permission was granted for the founding of a chantry in Haworth 'chapel', when Adam de Batteley (who had married Jane de Oxenhope and therefore owned the manor of Oxenhope) placed a surety on the souls of himself, his ancestors and certain relatives by giving a messuage, 7 acres of land and twenty shillings to augment the stipend of the curate, on condition that prayers be said, including some for 'those whose goods he had ill-gotten', 'every day'.

Many titled gentlemen, including Sir Alexander Emmott, presumably one of the Emmotts of Emmott Hall in Haworth, held the living of Haworth in the succeeding years, then in 1547, during the reign of Edward VI, the chantries were abolished by law, their revenue passing to the crown – and the curate of Haworth found himself in very straitened circumstances.

Eventually the people of Haworth, characteristically, decided that something must be done about this and that they themselves would do it. They collected £36, purchased land at Stanbury, and set up a trust, appointing Andrew Heaton and Christopher Holmes as first trustees, their 'heirs and successors' to follow in their footsteps. The income from this trust was to augment the stipend of the Haworth curate – but there were strings attached. The choice of the incumbent was to be at the discretion of the trustees and, once in office, if his behaviour should give rise to concern, then their financial support could be withdrawn and the money given to a worthy cause.

Thus, as a result of this Elizabethan trust dated 1559, the administration of Haworth Church has not always been straightforward, with wrangles often occurring between trustees and the ecclesiastical hierarchy, and Patrick Brontë himself once described it in a letter as 'great peculiarity of circumstance'.

The coming of William Grimshaw in 1742 was a case in point. The people of Haworth and the trustees had decided that they wanted Grimshaw; the vicar of Bradford, William Kennet, had other ideas. In the end, after a legal battle, Grimshaw came to Haworth and Haworth under him became one of the centres of the great Methodist Evangelical Revival. (In its early stages the Methodist movement was within the confines of the Established Church.)

Haworth parsons up to and including Grimshaw were not provided with a parsonage, and Grimshaw bought Sowdens himself the year he came to Haworth, leaving it to his son in his will. It was not until 1774 that the trustees bought 'Parson's Croft' – a field of roughly 'two days' work', or one acre, which was near

The interior of the old Brontë Church, showing the triple-decker pulpit from which William Grimshaw, John Wesley and Patrick Brontë preached.

the church – for £137, with the intention of building a parsonage on it. This was delayed, and four years later they bought another field, 'Halsteads', and work started immediately on building a parsonage there instead, the necessary finance coming from the trust. Much later, during Brontë's time, the Sunday School was built on Parson's Croft.

But the biggest confrontation of all arose in regard to the appointment of Patrick Brontë. In 1819 the vicar of Bradford, the Revd Henry Heap, went over the heads of the trustees and wrote to Patrick Brontë advising him that he was appointed to Haworth. Brontë was delighted – the trustees were incensed. They had known that his name had been put forward but were waiting to be consulted before it became official. In the summer of 1819 Patrick Brontë, innocent of the furore that had been caused, walked over to Haworth from Thornton to take a look at what he thought was his new parish. From Haworth he walked to Stanbury and introduced himself to Stephen Taylor, one of the trustees, as the new incumbent. The fat was properly in the fire. Stephen Taylor, however, liked what he saw of Brontë and advised him to write to Mr Heap, giving his resignation of the living of Haworth, then apply for it again in a few months' time when the matter had gone through the proper channels with the trustees.

Patrick Brontë must have wondered what on earth he was coming to in Haworth, but in the end did as Stephen Taylor suggested. Things appeared to be coming to a successful conclusion, Patrick looked all set for Haworth – and then the trustees made a great mistake and came up against a man whose mettle was a match for theirs any day – Patrick Brontë himself. Before the final appointment was made they suggested that they should come over to Thornton to hear him preach. Patrick gave full vent to his Irish temper.

'My aim has been, and always will be, to preach Christ, and not myself,' he wrote, and absolutely refused to 'preach to please'. The dispute continued throughout the year, with nobody in this three-cornered fight between Heap, Brontë and the trustees willing to give any ground, and eventually, probably in desperation, the vicar of Bradford made another mistake and appointed Samuel Redhead to the living instead, acting entirely on his own initiative once again.

Mr Redhead was already well known to the people of Haworth – he had often deputised during the illness of Mr Charnock, the last incumbent, and had sometimes taken services there while the living had been vacant after Charnock's death. The fact remained, however, that Redhead had been appointed without their consent, or the consent of the trustees, and they would have none of him. The trust had been violated and they showed their disapproval in no uncertain manner.

On the morning he was to conduct his first service after his appointment, the church was packed 'even to the aisles', with most of the congregation wearing clogs. During the reading of the second lesson they rose as a man and left the church to the accompaniment of as much clattering and banging as they could muster. Only Mr Redhead and his clerk remained to finish the service.

On the second Sunday the church was well filled but the aisles were carefully left clear, and at the same point in the service an uproar was created by the dramatic

The Black Bull, where Samuel Redhead found haven. Later Branwell Brontë also found solace here when his life became too difficult to cope with.

entrance of a half-witted man seated backwards on an ass with his head piled high with old hats. Round and round the aisles he rode, and poor Redhead finally had to abandon the service because of the noise and confusion.

He, too, must have been a man of spirit, and he decided to try for a third time. Just before the service started, the equally determined parishioners led to the front of the church a very sooty chimney-sweep, whom they had earlier reduced to a state of sublime intoxication. There he sat until Mr Redhead mounted the pulpit for the sermon and then, no doubt goaded by some mischief maker, he followed and tried to embrace the parson. A free-for-all followed and Redhead, this time in danger of serious assault, fled to the Black Bull from where he made an ignominious escape, his determination shattered.

Patrick Brontë was then invited once more to the living of Haworth, this time with the consent of all concerned, and the Brontë story as we know it was ensured. A few years later, Samuel Redhead was invited as guest preacher to Haworth and, brave man that he was, he accepted the invitation. On this occasion the congregation received him with great warmth – just to show that there was nothing personal in their previous treatment of him.

Today Haworth Church still has its trustees, and they still have the right to appoint the Rector and take action if he 'be negligent in his duties', as set out in the original Elizabethan document, but the Bradford Diocese has taken over many of their responsibilities. The last of the church land was sold about forty years ago and the proceeds invested in a Charity Trust, the income of which goes to the diocese. In 1983 Haworth Rectory on West Lane, originally built and maintained by the trustees, was sold to Bradford Diocese which now maintains it; the proceeds of this sale were also invested and the income again goes to Bradford Diocese. Thus, monies from the original trust still augment to a very large degree the stipend for the living of Haworth.

Life is now much more peaceful in Haworth, in this respect at least, although the characteristics that motivated the past are still there. One notices, too, that Haworth exerts a strange influence on those who have been its incumbents; they are most likely to return – to walk up the steep Main Street, or to preach, or to see friends. It is probably true to say that once you have been incumbent in Haworth, you are never quite the same again.

17

Nature's Gentleman

It seems to me I know the 'Old Gentleman' very well – in fact, once I almost met him. I was working in the old kitchen at Oldfield House very early one summer's morning – 2 a.m., in fact – when I heard footsteps, slow and measured, coming down the staircase he himself had installed. They walked past the kitchen door and along the passage to the front door – then they stopped. When I went to look there was nobody there – I'd just missed him.

James Mitchell came to Oldfield, about a mile above Ponden along the road to Oakworth, in 1820, after forty years spent in the care and study of trees. In his book *Dendrologia*, a natural history of trees, which he wrote while he was at Oldfield, he says, 'And now, Moses-like, after forty years wandering, I have retired to write my deuteronomy, or recital, not upon Mount Sinai, but to the Mountains in the West of Yorkshire, to enjoy the reward of temperance and industry.'

But unlike Moses he did rest in his promised land, for his grave is in a field between the house and the young River Worth, overlooking the little valley he loved so much. To the east, Haworth clings to its craggy hillside; to the west, Ponden Kirk guards the valley against Lancashire; and opposite, Stanbury straddles its long hill, very much as it did when James Mitchell gazed across to it. The 'Old Gentleman's Grave' stands on a grassy promontory – springs from the hillside form a guard of honour on either hand before they tumble down to meet the Worth, and a respectful gathering of trees appropriately gives shade and shelter to the little walled 'cemetery'. The headstone is inscribed 'In Memory of Mr James Mitchell, late Proprietor and Occupier of Oldfield House, who died on the 27th day of January, 1835, Aged 72 years', and besides it lies a giant stone, subject of some conjecture.

One story is that the Old Gentleman had the stone rolled from the house down towards the valley, and wherever it landed, there would he be buried. Considering the lie of the land, it is much more likely that a second story is the correct one. James Mitchell was an experienced landscape gardener and one day he and six labourers were bringing a cartload of stones up the valley from nearby quarries to build a rockery at Oldfield House. One of the stones was so huge that it could not be lifted on to the cart and had to be rolled up the hill instead, and when they reached the grassy mound the men were told to leave it there. Mystified, they did so, and when they reached the house Mr Mitchell gave them each a shilling, shared a seven-year-old gallon of ale between them, and said that when he died he wished to be buried where the stone rested. He also left instructions that a twig from each of the surrounding trees was to be put into the grave with him.

His instructions were carried out, and in 1835 hundreds attended his funeral, although the local church minister refused to conduct the service on unconsecrated ground and a Nonconformist minister officiated instead.

The 'Old Gentleman's Grave', with Stanbury on the skyline.

James Mitchell was born in London in 1762, but both his parents hailed from Yorkshire. Because he was a sickly child he was sent back to Yorkshire, to be reared in a vicarage at Halifax. The good Yorkshire air obviously worked wonders and eventually he started his career by becoming an apprentice to a nurseryman and planter in the West Riding, after which he returned to the south to work for four years at the dismantling of Enfield Chase in Middlesex, which he described as his 'Novitiate'.

Then for eleven years, as foreman for Eames and Webb, Newground Workmen and Landscape Gardeners, he worked in various places and estates in the south until he moved to Stanstead in Sussex where he acted as steward for ten years.

Stanstead Park was in a dilapidated condition when he arrived, and his work involved the demolition and rebuilding of farms and cottages, for which he drew up all the plans himself and supervised their construction, the management of thousands of acres of woodland, pasture and meadow, the marketing of timber and general administration. Great store seems to have been set on his initiative and judgement as his employer was 'too sensible of her own dignity ever to be degraded by placing herself between me and those I had to deal with' – so writes James Mitchell in *Dendrologia*. Philosophically, he also writes, 'Whoever place themselves between their agent and his patients draw a sluice that inundates the whole estate with anarchy and confusion – which destroy all subordination, not only among labourers but among the tenants and tradespeople, and create an abundant harvest for pettifoggers.' Obviously he and his employer had reached great understanding – equally obviously he was a strict disciplinarian, although he admits himself to acting under a 'wise and sound head'. Albeit, within seven years the restoration and reorganisation of Stanstead was complete, with 'not a gate wanting upon the whole estate'.

Eventually he moved on to pastures new, and spent the next nine years surveying and collecting notes and data from estates, parks and gardens all over the country, places such as Studley Park, Castle Howard, Chillingham Park, Kensington Gardens, Longleat and Woburn Park. The fruits of these labours are preserved in *Dendrologia*, together with a wealth of geographical, scientific and botanical knowledge, and although the author calls himself 'An Ignorant Philosopher', and in the best literary tradition of Chaucer makes excuses for his poor turn of phrase, he obviously revels in his own rhetoric.

His mentor was John Evelyn, who many years before in *Silva*, his own work on trees, declared that 'the business of planting is an art and there is nothing more becoming and worthy of a gentleman'. The dedication of *Dendrologia* is 'To the Immortal Shades and Manes of Messieurs John Evelyn, Nehemiah Grew and Stephen Hale', and is signed 'Your Ghostships' Debtor and Humble Admirer, Rural Rusticus'. James Mitchell was obviously not without a sense of humour.

It seems also that he was a man of some considerable wealth when he came to Oldfield in 1820, and was able to put his wide experience to good use there. In those days the property consisted of the original Oldfield House, built in 1667, barn, stable and other outbuildings, two attached cottages and several 'closes', or parcels of land, adjoining, as well as a stretch of Oakworth Moor with lead mining and quarrying rights. He marked his arrival at Oldfield House by making immediate changes to the property. One of the adjoining cottages was enlarged by the addition

Oldfield House (with the author's washing drying), c. 1980.

of elegant Georgian reception rooms along the east front, leaving the original part as a roomy farmhouse kitchen with old oak beams and mullioned windows. An equally elegant staircase was added, complete with coloured glass arched window, doors were made through into the original Oldfield House, and the whole became a large and imposing residence. (Years ago these doors were blocked up again – Oldfield House became 'semi-detached' – and in recent years the outbuildings have been developed to house even more families.) The date, 1820, was carved on the impressive stone gateposts at the top of the drive, and also on gateposts nearer the house, the gardens were landscaped and ornamental rockeries made and, naturally, many new trees were planted, some of which survive today.

And then, in September 1824, there was an occurrence that staggered the neighbourhood. According to James Mitchell, 'the thermometer in a cool room stood at 64 degrees; the atmosphere dense and gloomy; the clouds in the west, at three o'clock, changed to the colour of new sheet copper; from which issued most vivid lightning, with a tremendous single peal of thunder'. This was followed by torrential rain and a great upheaval on the moors above Wuthering Heights known as Crow Hill. The peaty crust of the soil burst open and bog water and 'ooze' poured down the Ponden Valley, enveloping the River Worth, sweeping away stone walls and anything in its path, damaging bridges, and choking up the waterwheels of mills and factories. Onward the murky torrent flowed into the River Aire just beyond Keighley, and it is recorded that the river water was useless for the dyers as far away as Leeds.

The 'Old Gentleman's Grave', Oldfield: James Mitchell's last resting place.

Patrick Brontë in his Haworth Parsonage saw it happen as he was anxiously scanning the moors for his children who had gone for a walk that afternoon. Fortunately they had 'found a place of shelter', but in his sermon the following Sunday he referred to the bog burst as a sign of the wrath of God and a warning to sinners! In his book James Mitchell refers more prosaically to the fact that some of his mature sycamores were killed by the 'cankery nature' of the flood water.

James Mitchell lived at Oldfield for fifteen years, during which time he wrote his book, tended his gardens, completed his alterations to the property and generally lived the life of a 'gentleman', which was regarded as an occupation in those days. He wore wooden pattens on his feet as he tramped round his demesne caring for his trees, firmly believing as he planted, pruned and planned that, like Laertes of old, he was making a stake in the future.

And finally he was laid to rest, as he dictated, on his own property in his chosen place. It is doubtful whether he had to cut through the 'red tape' that abounds today for the same privilege. Planning permission must now be sought, public notices of intent prominently displayed, possibly permission obtained from the Home Secretary – and the site must be at least 200 yards from the nearest dwelling and not within range of running water . . . so much for the springs from the hillside flowing into the River Worth.

And yet, having lived in his house for many years, I'm glad he rests where he does. Impossible to separate such a personality from the ripeness of his years . . . his influence lingers in the house, in the calm peace of the place, as surely as the wind still blows through the trees he planted here.

18

Stanbury and the School under the Sky

pproach Stanbury from Keighley and you feel you are climbing to the top of the world; look down on it from the path just below Wuthering Heights and the village on its hill looks like a green and grey castellated Cornish pasty sitting in the bottom of the valley. On either side are the River Worth and Sladen Reservoir, beyond them are ancient fields defined by drystone walls, and then the moors soar upwards, fold upon fold of bracken, bilberry, bog and heather.

Stanbury, 'stony hill', has clung to its own hilltop since before Domesday – and the stones are very much in evidence. 'Moor'ead rattlers' they called the coal produced by the short-lived Stanbury Coal, Iron and Lead Mining Co. Ltd over a century ago,

Stanbury village, from Hob Hill, at the beginning of the track leading to Top Withens.

and it has been said that you could have stoked up the fire with them on a Saturday, gone off to Morecambe for a week, and poked it into life again on your return. Not surprising that the company petered out when the railways brought better quality coal to the area. Robert-le-Smith was perhaps a precursor of the miners when in 1346 he was fined two pence for taking coal from his Lord's land, and even today traces of mines and spoil heaps can be found dotted about the Brontë moors.

After the Norman Conquest, Stanbury folk worked like ants from their hill, carting the De Lacy family goods along the trans-Pennine pack-horse route between Clitheroe and Pontefract, but by the end of the nineteenth century they were mostly smallholders, weavers, woolcombers or quarrymen, or sometimes a combination of several in order to eke out a living. Nearly every cottage had a hand-loom, and in old beams niches can still be seen where the looms were fastened; later, clogs clattered down the valley in the early mornings as villagers went to work at the mills at Ponden, Lumb Foot or Griffe. In those days two main factors in the development of the village were the excellent Co-operative Society, started in 1890, and the Brontë Bus Company a little later on.

Stanbury Co-op was the envy of its neighbours, with 'divi' sometimes double theirs though astute buying on the part of the manager. 'It were run on its own' – staunchly independent until 1967 when it amalgamated with Keighley and Skipton (the age of the supermarket had arrived), and in 1971 it closed altogether. In its heyday it was the centre of village life, organising public teas, concerts and galas; these galas featured 'knife and fork' teas, sports, processions and a brass band engaged for £8 plus tea, and in 1937 the magnanimous committee decided to give tea to the police controlling Gala Day traffic through the village. Today all that is left of the Co-op is a few disc checks owned by collectors and a hoist affixed to what is now a house in Main Street, and painted in black enamel to look 'ornamental'.

The Taylor family have been prominent in Stanbury since the sixteenth century, and Stephen Taylor was a friend of the Brontës. In fact, he and his sons George, Robert and John, in family tradition, were trustees of Haworth Church, and two of the seven wagons used by the Brontës when they moved to Haworth were loaned by the Taylors. The beautiful west window of Haworth Church, depicting the twelve apostles, was the gift of Mr G.S. Taylor when the church was rebuilt in 1881, and cleverly hidden in the design are likenesses of some of the Taylor family. When Mr Taylor died childless Stanbury Manor passed to his nephew, Charles Bairstow, and now Susan Green (née Bairstow) lives there with her husband and family. Susan, like her forebears, is one of the trustees of Haworth Church.

Drinking water used to be a problem at Stanbury, and before Sladen Reservoir was completed in 1925 it had to be piped across the valley to the village well-house, built by the Taylors. Even so, prudent housewives drew their water on Sunday for Monday washdays before it was reduced to a mere trickle.

William ('never Bill') Robinson lived in an idyllic cottage overlooking the reservoir with his wife Sally Ann. William, like his father and his uncle, was farm bailiff for the Bairstows, and the cottage was his 'legacy', rent-free for his lifetime. He worked on the Bairstow farm as a schoolboy. 'I could spread eighty piles of muck before I went to school, and eighty when I got back – at a ha'pennny a pile that wasn't bad going. Mind you, I used to ask 'em to leave me little piles,' confessed William. Sally Ann was an amazing lady renowned for her sponge cakes, although she rarely ate them herself. She kept her family supplied, they were in great demand at village fêtes and others were taken round the village as gifts. Sally Ann was

William ('never Bill') Robinson and his wife Sally Ann outside their cottage in Stanbury.

severely critical of her baking and was not happy unless the sponge cakes were absolute perfection, which they usually were.

William was not only President of Stanbury Co-op but also organist at the Wesleyan Chapel, which had to be closed in 1967 owing to 'dry rot and poverty'. When the chapel was built in 1832, however, it prospered so much that it was enlarged in 1845 and 1860 and was a power to be reckoned with in Stanbury. At one time Sunday afternoon gambling on Stanbury moors was a favourite pastime for some of the villagers, but the Wesleyans were on to them and often the gamblers were rounded up and brought along to the services.

One of these gamblers was called Jonas Sunderland, or more often 'Jonas O'Fines', and during a revival meeting was so moved that he changed not only his name but his ways and became a preacher of some note – thereafter he was called 'Salvation Jonas'. Of course, the highlight of the chapel year was the anniversary, with great emphasis being placed on the music and the money, and hospitality was offered to everybody who came to the village.

Now the chapel building has been refurbished to provide homes for 'off-comed'uns' and the revival meetings, the singing and the crowds are just echoes in the valley. William Robinson, who was so much involved in the village as it was, regretted the passing of time at Stanbury. 'When Stanbury were normal we used to gather at Kemp Wall to talk at night – now strangers and visitors sit on the seat outside the pub. There's not many of the "old lot" left – people are buying barns and doing them up.'

Halfway along Main Street, on the right-hand side of the road as you walk towards the moors, is a curious blocked-up doorway halfway up a house wall – a touching reminder of the Stanbury Quakers. These spiritual stalwarts used to meet here in an upper room from about 1656, using an outside stairway, after William Clayton, a handloom weaver, had walked to Bradford from Stanbury to hear George Fox, and had been won over by his preaching. His simple message had special appeal to these down-to-earth men of the moors, and soon took root in the village.

Initially the followers of George Fox were called 'Tremblers', although they feared no man, only God, the nickname arising from Fox's favourite exhortation that they should 'tremble at the Word of the Lord'. Later they became known as the Quakers, and they disliked both names equally, preferring rather the simple title of 'Friends of God'. Although the Quakers themselves were peace-loving people they seemed to attract violence and the Stanbury Quakers suffered for their beliefs.

William Clayton was at a Quaker meeting in Padiham in 1660 when 'there came the constable and the priest . . . and the priest laid vilant hands on me and pulled me down and out of the meeting . . .'. In November 1661 eight of them were committed to gaol at York 'with no beds' for eight nights for refusing to take the 'Oth of Aleagense', and they were committed for a further twelve weeks but 'in better rooms' for 'meeting together against the lawes of the nation'. Their refusal to take the 'Oth' was not political – they simply believed that truth was truth and the swearing of oaths therefore quite unnecessary.

There were many other instances of fines and imprisonment for the Stanbury Quakers but they were not daunted, and in 1670 obtained a lease of 'Horton Croft',

Haymaking at Stanbury, looking across the Worth Valley to Oldfield.

a small portion of land adjoining their Meeting Room, to be used as a burial ground. The lease was for 999 years and the annual rent was 1*d*. In 1710 it would seem that this lease was superseded by another one drawn up for a mere twenty-one years, but inflation had raised its ugly head – the annual rent this time was 2*s* 6*d*, to be paid at Pentecost. As the first recorded burial – that of a child – took place in 1656, there must have been an earlier arrangement for the use of Horton Croft by the Quakers, but their records were lost for many years. Eventually most of them came to light in an old chest in Liverpool, and these are now safely preserved at the Quaker headquarters in London. There were forty-five recorded interments in the little Croft, which is thought to be the oldest Quaker burial-ground in England, but a directive against memorials was issued at a Quaker meeting in 1717, and no monuments from that time onward have ever been found there.

Quakerism began to decline in the area after 1720, possibly to make way for that other spiritual giant, William Grimshaw, who burst upon the Haworth scene in 1742. The Stanbury Quakers slumber now, unmolested at last, beneath the fresh-blown grass of Horton Croft, and until recently the only visual evidence in the village of their ever having been there was the blocked-up doorway. Mrs Gladys Shackleton, former village schoolmistress, who lived in the old Meeting House and owned Horton Croft, decided she would like to do something to mark their last resting place, and now a plain and dignified stone cross has been set into the wall surrounding the Croft, by the side of the road through Stanbury. Its simple and

High jinks at a Stanbury pram race to celebrate the Queen's Silver Jubilee in 1977.

eloquent message is '1656–1718. 45 Quakers.' And so, all this long time after their struggles, a loving memorial has been raised to the faithfulness of the Stanbury Quakers – or perhaps they would prefer to be remembered simply as 'Friends'.

Another Stanbury reminder of stirring times is the top deck of the famous triple-decker pulpit from old Haworth Church, used by William Grimshaw, John Wesley and Patrick Brontë. It was rescued in a dilapidated state from a barn owned by the Taylors, and now stands in the little village church, built by Patrick Brontë, along the main road through the village.

Stanbury folk are tough – or at least they used to be. Nellie Hartley was thirteen in 1923 when she dodged an errand so that she could play on the small railway track which brought clay from the moors for the partially constructed Sladen Reservoir. While she was climbing on a bogey piled with iron rails, a friend inadvertently set it off, her coat caught in the wheels as she tried to jump off and the bogey ran over her hand, almost severing the thumb. Nellie, with her hand wrapped in her cap, was taken to a friend's house, where her friend's mother promptly fainted. Eventually Nellie reached her own home and her father decided they would have to walk into Haworth to see the doctor. Now the doctor was a kindly man. He gave Nellie a glass of milk and a piece of sponge cake – and told them to go to the hospital in Keighley, travelling by train to Ingrow and trackless trolley to Keighley – that is, if Father had enough train fare with him. 'I've got to go home first to change me clogs,' was Nellie's first thought, but thankfully reason prevailed. Father got the fare together, but as they were boarding the train at Haworth big sister got off – and Nellie got her face slapped for being a nuisance.

At Ingrow Nellie refused to get on the new-fangled trolley, so they walked over another mile to the hospital. The thumb was stitched on again – a masterpiece of surgery at that time – Nellie spent thirteen weeks in hospital and bore the scars of her escapade all her life.

In 1890 Jonas Bradley came to teach at Stanbury, and put the little school and the village on the map with his methods of teaching nature study. The scholars had a heyday, wandering the moors in search of botanical specimens to collect and draw, and the school inspectors complained because there was never anybody 'at home' when they called. Teachers and reporters blazed a trail to the school to observe Jonas Bradley's methods, and he was sought out by scholars, statesmen and film directors. The school corresponded with places such as South Africa and Australia, and botanical specimens were exchanged and sometimes planted in the tiny school garden. Jonas himself wrote articles for leading national newspapers and lectured all over the country, including London, and in April 1903 the *Royal Magazine* called his school 'The School under the Sky'.

Scar Hill, above Stanbury. A small railway ran up here to bring clay for the puddle trench of Sladen Reservoir.

His log books, written mostly in his own spidery writing, give the occupations of the fathers of his pupils – fariner, warp-dresser, stone merchant, grinder, quarryman, navvy, waterworks manager, cartwright, engine tenter – thus telling a lot about the life and times in the area, and they also provide a wealth of information on current affairs and interesting people who visited the school.

1901: Sept. 20.   Capt. Brownrigg of the Imperial Light Horse, who returned from the front in the transport 'Wakool' on Friday last, gave the children a description of journeys to America (buying horses for the British Government in the Rockies) and then to Cape Colony, Natal, Transvaal etc.

1902: June 3.   Peace is proclaimed. (This, of course, referred to the Boer War and was followed by an account of village festivities.)

1902: June 25.   I am instructed by the Board to state that the permission to close the School on Thursday and Friday next is withdrawn. This is in consequence of the Coronation Festivities having been postponed indefinitely – the King having undergone an operation for appendicitis.

1910: Nov. 30.   Two noted people died this morning . . . Mrs Ratcliffe, sister of Martha Brown, servant of the Brontës, and Timmy Feather, the hand-loom weaver – aged respectively 76 and 85 years.

1911: Sept. 3.   This afternoon we dug up 60 lbs of potatoes.

1911: Dec. 15.   Rowland Cragg, journalist from Manchester Guardian, visited school – paid visits several times before.

1914: May 15.   Lower Laithe (Sladen Reservoir) Very soon the puddle trench will begin to be filled in – first with concrete (narrow lower portion) and then with clay.

1915: April 28.   Children knitting scarves, helmets, socks for soldiers. Mr Pighills, Sun Street, Keighley, also acknowledges receipt of 479 eggs collected by children for wounded soldiers and sailors. 'Bravo, Stanbury,' he says.

If the children's knowledge of the 'three Rs' suffered, they certainly had their horizons widened, and morning assemblies were often enlivened with a glance through the morning papers.

Jonas Bradley was a founder member of the Brontë Society and a great authority on the Brontës, often to be seen sitting in front of the Brontë Museum having a 'rick o' bacca' before meeting some important visitor. His home was open house, and Halliwell Sutcliffe was a frequent visitor, writing his *Ricroft of Withens* there. His energy was boundless, he was an avid photographer (William Robinson, who was his pupil, cleaned slides for him during school hours), he lectured on such topics as 'London, the Sunny South and Boulogne before the War' as well as local ones, and not only led Haworth Ramblers on arduous walks but prepared pamphlets and lectured about the route as they walked.

Egocentricity was one of his failings. One old Stanbury resident remembered being in the village post office and listening to someone using the public telephone. She could not see who it was, but a eulogy was being delivered on Jonas Bradley and his accomplishments, apparently for some newspaper. The old lady waited to see who this admirer of Jonas Bradley might be, and when the caller appeared it was Jonas Bradley.

Another old lady remembered, as a girl, visiting Jonas in his home during his later days at Stanbury. An old cooking-pot of stew was on continual simmer on his stove and was 'never bottomed'. From time to time, gifts of a ham bone, an onion, etc. would be thrown into the pot and given a good stir, and then at the appointed hour Jonas would scoop out a bowlful for his meal. Mementoes of past dinners decorated the front of his waistcoat, and that he escaped food poisoning is a miracle.

Jonas Bradley was larger than life, eccentric, with a weakness for whisky, and his ways were not always approved of by some villagers, yet he made a colourful contribution to life in the area.

The old back lane through Stanbury, where time seems to have stood still.

Two roads lead through Stanbury. One is the little old forgotten track looking over to Oldfield, rarely used, peaceful, a distillation of times past. Once it led underneath where Sladen Reservoir now stands and up the other side of the valley to Stanbury Heights. The other road is comparatively new, and in summer hikers and residents continually leap out of the way of the tangle of tourist traffic and modern farm machinery.

Together these two roads present a picture of Stanbury as it is today.

19

The Many Sides of Sir Isaac

To most people today Oakworth is just a station on the Worth Valley Steam Railway line, but up the hill and away from Haworth there is a village that people flocked to well over a century ago. Before the Brontë 'shrine' was really established, it was Oakworth that attracted the tourists, and the man behind it all was Isaac Holden, Member of Parliament, lecturer, industrialist, inventor, philanthropist, baronet – and creator of the 'eighth wonder of the world'.

Isaac Holden was born on 17 May 1807, near Glasgow; his father was a coal-miner, and both his parents were staunch Wesleyans. They were keen for him to be educated, he was anxious to contribute to the family income, and consequently pleased both sides by working in the mills during the day and studying at evening classes and often late into the night as well. The pattern was set for his lifetime of hard work.

Eventually he became a teacher, and while at the Reading Academy he produced his first invention, of necessity. He was in the habit of getting up at four o'clock in the morning to study, which often meant fumbling about in the dark with flint and tinder to produce a light. This waste of time irked him and, characteristically, he decided to do something about it – he invented the Lucifer safety match. One day while delivering a science lecture he demonstrated his 'find', thereby kindling more interest than he bargained for, and soon Lucifers were being produced commercially by someone else. Isaac had never applied for a patent as he thought it was wrong to cash in on an idea come by as the result of a 'happy thought'.

He was fascinated by the business of mills, however, and soon left teaching to go as bookkeeper to Townend Bros, worsted manufacturers, at Cullingworth near Bradford. As a child he had been considered 'feeble', and had become a fanatic about matters of personal health – 'habitual exercise in the open air . . . and severe discipline in reference to everything' was his code for living. And he only accepted the job with Townend Bros on condition that he be allowed two hours' exercise in the fresh air every day, from 7 a.m. to 8 a.m. and from 11 a.m. to noon, to be taken in lieu of holidays. The condition was granted, and soon he became mill manager and then a partner in the firm, all the time keeping strictly to his exercise programme. 'I never stopped in for the weather, neither for snow, hail nor rain, and it did not matter whether it was hot or cold, I never shortened my walks. That lays the foundation of youth in old age.

Sir Isaac Holden, Member of Parliament, lecturer, industrialist, inventor, philanthropist – and creator of the 'eighth wonder of the world'.

Then my diet was always sparing – I never varied more than a few pounds in weight . . . I kept down to eight stone six pounds . . . if I began to get heavier I cut off supplies.'

Isaac often worked from 6 a.m. until 11 o'clock at night, and sometimes persuaded Edward Townend to walk with him over three miles to Keighley and back, in all weathers, to attend lectures at the Mechanics' Institute. Sometimes he went alone, and kept a high regard for the work done by the Mechanics' Institute all his life.

Among all this Isaac married Marion Love of Paisley, adapted and improved the early wool-combing machines at Townends, and also introduced a new genappe yarn. Again he had difficulty with patents, as the Townends would have nothing to do with them, and finally he gave his notice, but stayed on for a year until three men could be trained to take his place!

Then he went into partnership with his friend, Samuel Lister of Manningham (later to become Lord Masham), and although other firms, including Townends, were using his genappe yarn to advantage long before he and Lister obtained a patent, their firm prospered. They established mills in France for merino wool and Isaac brought out his own 'square motion' woolcombing machine.

A deeply religious and caring man, he worried at first that his machine would spoil what had been a cottage industry, but was eventually convinced that it created jobs in other branches of the textile trade – a theory borne out by the French enterprises which worked day and night during the American Civil War, manufacturing cloth for uniforms and producing high employment figures and even higher profits.

When Sam Lister retired, the firm became Isaac Holden and Sons (the sons being Angus and Edward), and Isaac himself became renowned as a public benefactor in Oakworth, Keighley and Bradford. He gave generously to Methodist chapels, staunchly supported the Liberal Party which he represented in Parliament, was instrumental in having a new Mechanics' Institute built in Keighley, and when, seventeen years later, a new wing was added, it was his £2,000 that made it possible. He endowed scholarships, gave to Bradford Technical College and recreational projects, and donated £1,000 to Oakworth to establish its own Mechanics' Institute. One tenth of his income was given away.

Alongside this and his business, he maintained his daily outdoor exercise and meagre diet, often living for a month at a time on nothing but fruit, avoiding cereals and root vegetables which 'abound in lime', occasionally permitting himself three ounces of 'flesh meat' for lunch, bathing scientifically, never drinking with his food and thus retaining 'the vigour of the saliva' – all he recommended for those 'on the shady side of forty'. In his eighties he had been known to walk all the way from Oakworth to his Bradford business in the snow, and then refuse the offer of a carriage to take him into the city centre.

This mixture of hard work, philanthropy and masochism paid dividends and Isaac Holden, created Baronet in 1893, lived in robust good health to be ninety, but it is for the creation of his house at Oakworth, and for its amazing grounds, that he will be long remembered.

Oakworth House started as a modest affair, the home of Isaac Holden's second wife's brother (his first wife died in 1847), and Isaac bought it against his better judgement to please his wife. Having acquired it, however, he applied his personal philosophy – something good must be made out of it. He therefore set about a colossal scheme of expansion and improvement, until there was very little of the original building left. But instead, a building of rare and costly elegance had materialised, filled with works of art from all over the world and tastefully decorated and appointed under the direction of French craftsmen. Rare china, inlaid furniture, costly carpets, fine paintings and statuettes, Swiss wood carving, and ceilings decorated with gold graced the lovely rooms.

In contrast with his other spartan ideals, Isaac Holden believed that houses, particularly bedrooms, should be kept at an even warm temperature, although the air should be fresh, and 7,000 feet of 4 inch piping from the boilers assured a temperature of 60° throughout, while a clever arrangement of ventilation shafts changed the air every half hour. To provide water for the heating boilers, which also sustained the greenhouses and Turkish baths (Isaac Holden was a strong proponent of hydrotherapy), three small reservoirs had been built in the grounds of Oakworth House.

Among all this splendour was a bookcase containing about four dozen silver presentation trowels and mallets, used by Isaac Holden in the laying of foundation stones of various public buildings – a tribute to his busy public life. There was also the silver spade and the barrow used by him when, as Chairman of the new Worth Valley Railway Company, he cut the first sod when the railway was being built in 1864.

But if the house was remarkable, the surrounding gardens were even more so. Landscaped down to the last boulder, caves with labyrinthine 'walks', waterfalls and passages had been created, complete with 'fossil' tree trunks fashioned out of concrete by French artists 'in such a manner as to deny all but the closest scrutiny'. Water splashed over the rocks and trickled along ledges bordered by ferns and rare plants; staircases twisted between the 'walks', mirrors enlarged and repeated the vistas to infinity, and at night the whole was spotlighted by electricity generated by a gas engine.

The winter gardens were the crowning glory. Built at a cost of £30,000, which included blasting of bedrock to form a level surface, they extended to half an acre, were completely covered in glass and surmounted by a magnificent stained-glass dome. From the solid rock at one end, man and nature had combined to create caves and recesses, and a cascade of water leapt into a clear pool. About 1,000 yards of fine mosaic pavements circled flower-beds which contained rare and beautiful plants, including banana, orange, vine, peach and melon, as well as many varieties of orchid, and a dozen boilers and tens of thousands of feet of piping kept them at the right temperature. Joining on to these winter gardens was a magnificent billiard room, 30 foot square, which had cost £3,000 to build.

Stretching beyond the winter gardens, caves and greenhouses were about 30 acres of parkland, set out with flower borders, trees, shrubs and secluded walks, and behind the parkland were woods, farmland and three farms.

Having created this wonder, Isaac Holden had no wish to keep it to himself. His gardens and parklands were freely opened to the public, who came in droves to marvel at it, and nothing pleased him more than to wander along the miles of pathways and chat with his visitors.

All that was a long time ago, and there is not much left of former glory in what is now Oakworth Park. A plaque at the gateless entrance commemorates its heyday, statuettes top the gateposts, and to the right is a little 'rustic' concrete summer-house. The house has long since disappeared, partly pulled down, partly burned

Oakworth House, home of Sir Isaac Holden, which stood on the site of the present park.
The glass dome of the winter gardens and the chimney for the heating boiler are to the rear.
On the right is the old Methodist Chapel.

The fountain in Oakworth Park with the porch (the only remaining part of Oakworth House) in the background. In the foreground is a broken mosaic pavement at the entrance to the caves.

down, soon after Sir Isaac died in 1897. Only the imposing entrance porch is left, but this now leads straight on to a bowling green, which is presided over by a bronze bust of 'Isaac Holden MP' embellished with graffiti.

Behind the bust stands a marble fountain 'Erected by the Inhabitants of Oakworth as a token of Affectionate Respect for Sir Isaac Holden Bart. 1807 to 1897'; it is out of order and covered with more graffiti. The winter gardens are gone, the park flower-beds forlorn, only a small remnant of broken mosaic pavement remains behind the fountain, leading into the caves.

Yet to children in particular Oakworth Park still has a strange magic, a hint of fantasy. Although the caves are slightly smelly, they are exciting, kindling the imagination, and the stairways and balconies are places of adventure. Along one of the walks is a little sanctuary of my own childhood – a concrete 'rustic' wishing-well and chair.

Like all places of faded splendour, there is a feeling of decay in Oakworth Park; it is like a stage long unused – and with the principal actor gone for ever.

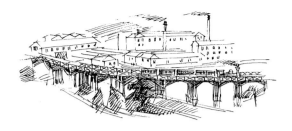

20

Steam Up in the Worth Valley

Escorted by an immaculately uniformed Station Superintendent, complete with peaked cap, gold braid and kid gloves, I felt like the Queen. Doors were opened, questions answered and everything of interest pointed out and explained.

The following day was not so Right Royal. Clad in a pair of old overalls and regulation cap, I shovelled coal into a blazing furnace and then held on to grimy handrails as I rattled along at a dizzy 12 mph – enjoying every minute of it. I was spending a weekend with the Worth Valley Railway and my culminating ride on the footplate of a steam engine must have been every little boy's dream – and every parson's, too, from what I can gather of the hobbies of members of 'the cloth'.

There's nothing quite like the acrid smell of a steam railway – that blend of sulphur, tar and hot oil (very evident when you are actually shovelling coal into the fire-box) that takes you back to more leisurely times when a ride on a train was an occasion.

My 'iron steed' was 'Hamburg', a 1903 vintage tank engine, usually called a 'kettle' in the trade, and the fact that I'd just signed an indemnity accepting full responsibility for my own possible demise should I fall out (I was told it was just an insurance formality) detracted not one jot from my experience, although there did seem to be very little between me and the railway lines. 'Hamburg' served its time on the Manchester Ship Canal and could actually rattle along at about 40 mph. It was named after one of its link ports and at the start of the First World War the name-plate was ripped from its side by anti-German demonstrators, who also threw the driver into the canal, even though the poor man happened to be British.

Our steam trip was in winter and took us from Oxenhope to Haworth and back again – at that time of the year the full line from Oxenhope to Keighley was only run by direct rail bus – but never has familiar countryside looked so exciting as seen from that swaying footplate. It was a cold and snowy day, but I felt warm as toast. 'It's just the job for a winter's day,' I shouted to the driver and fireman, as they manipulated levers and watched dials intently. 'Aye, not so bad today,' the driver shouted back, 'but when there's a cross-wind you get freezing ankles and red-hot ears – it's not so good then.' I was fascinated by a large Brasso tin standing on a shelf above the furnace. 'What's in there?' I asked. 'Brasso, of course,' came the reply. 'It

A Worth Valley steam train approaching Mytholmes tunnel from Oakworth.

was frozen solid this morning, so we're just thawing it out.' It gave the cab a homely appearance, and later the beautiful brass levers and knobs would be polished with pride by these amateur railway enthusiasts.

It was in April 1867 that the Keighley and Worth Valley Railway first opened, a belated result of the railway mania that gripped England in the 1840s. Various earlier plans had been mooted as the expanding railway companies jockeyed for power; one of the proposed lines would actually have finished in Haworth churchyard, which would have been quite some gradient. Fortunately it came to naught. Another was to run from Keighley, through Haworth, Hebden Bridge and so to Manchester, one of the promoters being Patrick Brontë. His daughters also invested part of Aunt Branwell's legacy in the York and North Midland Railway, with disastrous results.

John McLandsborough, the railway engineer, had a previous idea of running the line from Haworth to Stanbury, where it would divide. One branch would follow the Worth and then over to Colne, the other passing where Sladen Reservoir now stands, and up the Sladen Valley towards Brontë Waterfalls, presumably to transport stone from the quarries, and also coal, as several shafts were being worked at Stanbury on a small scale. It was also whispered that he'd heard there was gold 'in them thar 'ills'. This turned out to be pyrites, in very small quantities, so it was just as well that this plan, too, aborted.

Finally, in 1862, a group of local worthies formed the Keighley and Worth Valley Railway Company, and on Shrove Tuesday, 9 February 1864, after prayers were said by the Revd John Wade, there was a ceremonial cutting of the first sod by Isaac Holden, who had been elected chairman – it looked like full steam ahead. But not for long. Innumerable difficulties occurred before the railway finally opened in 1867.

While constructing a tunnel just above Ingrow, the navvies, working by the light of tallow candles, cut into a bed of quicksand, thereby causing a landslide, and the newly built Wesley Place Chapel, standing just above the tunnel, tottered with the subsidence. Ironically, Isaac Holden had laid the chapel's foundation stone only two years earlier. A new chapel was eventually built further back from the line, and it was four years before the trustees were awarded £1,980 damages. The cost of the new chapel was £3,000 but for 3s 0d.

Also, at Oakworth a row of houses had to be bought and the middle ones demolished for the line to pass through, a new row being built in compensation alongside the railway. The results of this demolition can still be seen in the strangely sawn-off appearance of a house just below the railway in Station Road.

But the strangest hold-up of all occurred again near Oakworth Station when a cow ate the plans while the surveyor's back was turned. Difficulties also arose when the Bridgehouse Beck happened to be in the wrong place and had to be diverted between Oxenhope and Haworth, and in November 1866 storms washed away 40 feet of banking at Damems, leaving the rails suspended in space. It says much for the determination of the Worth Valley folk that their railway ever got built at all.

When it did come the face and form of the valley changed. More mills sprang up along its length, with elegant mill-owners' houses, particularly in Oxenhope, and the farmers welcomed it for the transporting of milk and livestock. Haworth changed its shape, spilling down into the valley and up the other side as rows and rows of terraced houses were built on Browside for the mill workers.

The railway was owned by the company, but operated by Midland Railway, which eventually took it over in 1881 – thereby inheriting a headache at the same time. Initially it had been built on a tight budget, and by 1881 timber and cast iron were rotting and things falling apart in general, and money had to be poured in to bring it up to scratch. In 1891 work was started to do away with the rickety wooden trestle viaduct across Vale Mill Dam, just outside Oakworth, involving plans for a new cutting through Mytholmes Hill, but these had to be changed to a tunnel when blue clay was discovered. Five new bridges were necessary because of this change of route, and provision was made for a double track rail during reconstruction with an eye to a prosperous future.

The railway had its heyday during the first part of the twentieth century when four clerks and two ticket collectors were employed at Haworth and the stationmaster wore a frock coat. Then came the decline in rail use and on 30 December 1961 the last passenger train ran under British Rail on the Worth Valley line.

Immediately a murmur began among railway enthusiasts – the line must be preserved – and in March 1962 the Keighley and Worth Valley Railway Preservation Society was formed. Again a long period had to elapse between instigation and operation (six years this time) but in June 1968 the Worth Valley Line reopened.

The Society has flourished and its keenness, efficiency and friendliness might well be copied by certain major concerns running on very similar lines. Members come from all parts of the country, not just singly but in families, and 'once the bug's bitten, then that's it – they're with us for life'. All work is done voluntarily, but professional discipline is maintained of necessity, and it shows. A rigid staff roster is

Vale Mills old railway trestle viaduct, long since demolished as unsafe. (Reproduced courtesy of the Heaton family)

Oakworth Station. It was used as the location for filming The Railway Children, *and retains an immaculate early Edwardian image.*

drawn up monthly, and strictly adhered to, and for some jobs an examination has to be passed. There is an enthusiasm that is catching and everyone, from the shop assistants to the stationmasters, seems eager to talk about 'their' railway – endlessly. At Oxenhope the stationmaster sat me in an armchair in his office in front of a roaring fire (a similar fire burned in the general waiting-room), supplied me with a mug of hot tea, and talked proudly about the working atmosphere that pervades the Society – 'professional but friendly' was how he described it.

The Worth Valley Railway has six stations – Keighley, Ingrow, Damems, Oakworth, Haworth and Oxenhope – and with the exception of Oakworth the 'era' of the line is the 1950s, which happened to be a hardwearing, easy-to-maintain decade. Oakworth Station, however, takes a bigger step back in time and is strictly early Edwardian. This happened quite naturally, because two years after the line reopened the station was used for the filming of *The Railway Children*, and was refurbished appropriately for the year 1910. When the filming was over it was decided that the station looked so attractive it might as well remain that way, and it is a fascinating experience just to look round it, quite apart from travelling on the steam train. Everything is authentic and functional, from the fly-paper suspended from the ceiling to the old trolleys loaded with trunks and milk churns and the hand-operated fire-engine which is now used for watering the flower-beds. One rather grim detail – there is even a coffin and stretcher trolley, and an ancient platform-ticket machine (slight concession here), which has been converted to decimal coinage of necessity. The station has no electricity, only gas lighting, and the ladies' waiting-room is complete with carpet, uncut moquette sofa, and table with chenille cloth and aspidistra. On the wall are two large advertisements of the era: one, with two bathing belles suitably covered over, asks, 'What are the wild waves saying? Try Beechams Pills. Worth a guinea a box.' The ladies' toilet is tiled, immaculate and functional. 'Go in and have a plunge,' I was invited, 'it's quite remarkable. When Brian Johnston was here for *Down Your Way*, he was quite taken with it.' Outside, the platform and its embellishments look scrubbed and cared-for, with neat flower-beds, gleaming gas lamps and more old advertisements welded to the painted railings.

Next station down the line is Damems, its one claim to fame being that it is very small indeed. There is a local joke about a farmer who was caught taking the waiting-room away on the back of his cart. 'Nay,' he said, 'I thowt it were a 'en 'ut I'd been waiting t'delivery of.' Between Damems and Keighley is Ingrow Station, now groomed for stardom with its locomotive museum and 'one of the best carriage museums in the country'. It boasts its own telephone exchange and its dapper station building was physically moved from Foulridge near Colne.

At Oxenhope Station a gigantic carriage shed and carriage works have been built, and the stock museum has a prosperous look (the Society is now in a position to pick and choose what it takes on), but what really caught my fancy was a luxury saloon coach complete with armchairs, kitchen and toilet. It was built especially for a locomotive superintendent of the NER – you could say it was the predecessor of the company car – and it used to have its own special engine. It was given to the Society by a member who was a former employee of British Rail. On his retirement he was to be presented with a gold watch, but asked instead for the coach, and his request was granted. It has become known as 'The Old Gentleman's Coach', as it featured prominently in *The Railway Children*. In fact, the Society owes much of its prosperity to that film; about a week after its release, business 'just rocketed' – the week before the release it was running two coaches, the following week it was running six!

The attraction of the Worth Valley line to film companies is that it has everything – mills, factories, sewage beds, allotments, tunnels, level crossings; some of it is by no means picturesque in the accepted sense, yet it is a microcosm of the West Riding, from mills to moors.

With the price of the special smokeless coal for ever on the increase and the coal itself difficult to source, the Society still prospers. A large new engine shed has recently been built at Haworth, complete with inspection pit – 'before we had that it was a case sometimes of just lying in the snow under engines and working' – the repair workshops are well equipped and can tackle most heavy engineering jobs, and the stockyards are full of engines of every conceivable shape and size, weighing on average 100 tons, some of them with wheels like planets.

A double-headed 'Christmas Special' on the Worth Valley line climbing the gradient out of Haworth.

Several years ago, to improve the frequency of trains on a single track, a 'passing loop' was constructed near Damens by volunteers from the Society, and a complete signal-box was transported from Frizinghall by road, causing considerable excitement as it passed through the towns. Albert Modley had been its operator at Frizinghall before he went on the boards.

Each year the crowds come to the railway, drawn irresistibly by nostalgia and the spell of steam, taking photographs, waving out of windows, excited by what was taken for granted not so very long ago. In these days when modern trains are fast and featureless, and most stations apathetic and dreary, it is refreshing to visit the Worth Valley, where railway mania is still very much in evidence – and definitely contagious.

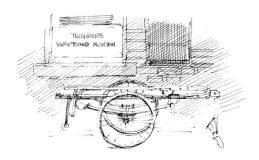

21

Cool, Calm and Collected

T he three reservoirs of the Upper Worth Valley hang like a triple pendant on the breast of the moors – Watersheddles, Ponden and Sladen (which is often called Lower Laithe). Watersheddles, the highest, is in Lancashire about 100 yards past the Yorkshire boundary, and, as the name suggests, draws its supplies from the bleak moorlands common to both counties – areas of peat bog where the peewit, the skylark and the grouse share their domain with impassive moorland sheep. Strange standing stones and rock formations straddle these moors and, only a short broomstick-ride away, Pendle Hill, haunt of the Lancashire witches, dominates the western skyline. Completed in 1877, Watersheddles is the cradle of the River Worth, often rocked by fierce winds and gales. During the First World War it was patrolled by local Boy Scouts, as rumour had it that the Germans intended to poison this main source of the Worth Valley domestic water supply. What this Dad's Army in embryo would have done had the Germans actually got up to any tricks is open to conjecture – but presumably they would have been prepared. Although Watersheddles is in Lancashire, just, it is the property of the Yorkshire Water Authority.

At the edge of the watershed, at dramatic Ponden Kirk (Penistone Crag of *Wuthering Heights*), countless streams combine to leap down into the valley. Here, two-thirds of the water is channelled back to Watersheddles by conduit, while a regulation one-third assumes comparative tranquillity as the Ponden Clough Beck, entering the second of the reservoirs, Ponden, in close harness with the young River Worth, which has taken its own course from Watersheddles down a narrow ravine.

Although the Worth Valley reservoir system was planned partly as a result of the droughts which hit Keighley in the 1860s, when private water pumps were thrown open for general use, mill owners allowed their dams to be used by the public and 'water was fetched in buckets, cans, carts and waggons to supply the wants of different parts of the town', Ponden Reservoir was not initially for domestic water consumption. It was opened in 1876 as a 'compensation' reservoir, and ensured a regular water supply to the mills which had sprung up along the Worth Valley; a legal agreement was made between the water authorities and a committee of mill owners that one-third of the water would be run off daily from the reservoir for the benefit of the mills – sluices were opened morning and evening and a statement of the volume of water in transit had to be given to the committee. Water was the life-blood of the valley.

Sladen Reservoir, with contemplative cat.

Today the mills lower down the valley are powered by electricity (although the sluices are still opened occasionally 'to maintain the life of the stream'), and some have forsaken the worsted industry for other products – plastics etc. But above Haworth the valley is peaceful, the mills have either disappeared or stand in ruins, bramble-covered, forlorn reminders of the days when the clatter of machines, and clogs, and the voices of working men and women mingled with the noise of running water. (One exception is the old cotton mill at Ponden, regenerated to sell household textiles, caneware, and so on.)

Times were even more stirring during the actual building of Ponden and Watersheddles Reservoirs, when over three hundred navvies lived in wooden huts in the area, or in rented accommodation. They were mainly hard, rough men, tackling a hard, rough job, but they brought a degree of prosperity with them. Stanbury shopkeepers never managed to 'put anything by' until the navvies came, and one man at Scar Top took in fourteen lodgers at 13*s* 6*d* each per week for 'Tommy' (navvies' slang for food) plus a quart of beer a day, probably illegally brewed. Masons and delvers, joiners, blacksmiths and labourers – the moors swarmed with men and horses; tramways, trucks and pumping engines ploughed up the peat and heather; and almost every house and farm did a little brewing 'on the side' to cater for the perpetual thirst of the navvies.

At Scar Top, William and Robert Heaton opened a brewery at a most propitious time, and needless to say it flourished. By 1877 they were using about 450 barrels, some up to 60 gallon capacity, and they advertised their 'Mild, bitter and pale ales, porters and stout, with light and other ales for table use, from 10*d* per gallon' over a wide area. Unfortunately, when the reservoirs were finished and most of the navvies left the area, with three pubs in Stanbury village, the brewery went bust!

The navvies were a full-blooded breed, as court records of the time show, and after a petition by Stanbury folk, Keighley was moved to send an extra constable on a bicycle 'to keep the navvies in order'. Petty theft was rife – Miles Pickles, the harassed landlord of the Cross Inn, Stanbury, had his coat stolen, for which the thief was sentenced to a month's hard labour (little change from navvying!). But rough as they were, their ladies were more than a match for them. Matilda Goddard, alias Hilda Thompson, alias Peniston, alias Wilson, is on record as having hit her former lover, Thomas Evans, over the head with a pint pitcher at Stanbury.

The navvies loved a good funeral and always made an effort to attend in their best clothes. They were also generous. John William Davies, on his way from Northampton to Ponden to work on the reservoir, called at a Stanbury pub for bread and cheese – then promptly died. The navvies paid for his funeral, although he had not even started on the job.

The lynchpin of all reservoir building was the puddle-trench, a massive membrane that stretched inside the embankment to prevent water from seeping underneath it. The foundations of the trench were dug down to solid rock, sometimes 20 or 30 feet deep, and it was at this time that most of the accidents happened; some of them were fatal. (At Ponden a large stone weighing 11 pounds fell on the head of Greenwood Hird while he was loading a truck with stones, and he died instantly.) A base of solid concrete was laid in the trench, a timber frame constructed, and then the trench was filled in with puddle or clay which never set completely, thus giving the embankment slight flexibility under stress. Clay for the puddle-trench was usually brought from the moors on small, single-track railways.

There was, too, a gentler side to the navvies. Some were keen botanists and at weekends would search the countryside for gentian roots to cook with their beef (their great passions were said to be beef, bacon and strong drink, not necessarily in that order), while one man who had been a sailor sometimes took his hard-living companions on to the moors at night to explain the wonders of the stars to them.

Eventually work was finished at Watersheddles and Ponden Reservoirs and in March 1877 celebratory dinners were held for local dignitaries and navvies – separately – the toast being 'Success to the Keighley Waterworks and prosperity to the town of Keighley'. Most of the navvies moved on, like an army, to new constructions, but a few stayed in the Worth Valley and married and raised families, as shown by the records at Stanbury School. Comparative peace reigned once more, although in 1891 a minor ripple occurred, water-wise, when the Oldfield Treatment Plant was constructed to purify the water from Watersheddles Reservoir and remove a tendency to lead poisoning caused by the action of the acid in moorland water on lead pipes.

Then in 1912 the navvies and engineers moved into the valley once more, this time lower down at Sladen – the final stage of the great Worth Valley Waterworks scheme was about to commence. Originally it was planned to build this reservoir further up the Sladen Valley (a tributary of the Worth) just below Bully Trees Farm, but the sedimentary rock there was found to be unsuitable.

Another puddle-trench, another railway line on to the moors, almost to Wuthering Heights, where faint traces of it can still be seen. A navvies' lodging-house came into being at Haworth with 'Beds 2*d* per night – good beds 3*d*' (although 'residents' were expected to do their own washing and cooking) and a large, tin Navvies' Mission Hall was built on West Lane, near where the entrance to the museum car park is now. This Mission Hall produced the first Haworth Boy Scout Troop as the navvies were joined by their wives and families. Then came the First World War, and work on the reservoir was postponed. When it started again after the war costs had more than doubled, but in 1925 Sladen Reservoir was completed – Keighley had another source of drinking water. The lower end of the Sladen Valley had been flooded by the reservoir, and a small worsted mill, footpaths and bridges had been submerged. Waterhead Lane, the old pack-horse track from Stanbury Heights to Stanbury Village, had dipped beneath the water, and Smith Bank Cottages and Farm along its track had been demolished – they would have teetered on the brink of the reservoir and therefore been unsafe. The green valley had become a great sheet of water, changing colours with the sky.

Mr and Mrs Dennis, the minister and his wife, at the Navvy Mission Hall on West Lane.

Comparatively recently another farm was demolished by the water authorities just below Sladen Reservoir to make way for more equipment. Ancient Dale Moor Farm, better known locally as 'Dollymoor', had been the home of clockmakers from about 1710 to 1850. Michael, Caleb and John Heaton lived there in 1771 or thereabouts, and in addition to clocks they made fiddles and other wooden instruments, as well as doing a little dentistry and doctoring on the side. Their sister Martha married a Jonas Barraclough, and their descendants followed the clockmaking tradition, eventually leaving Dollymoor and spreading to other parts of the area, including Leeds and Thornton. Zerrubabel, their grandson, launched out into the cork leg manufacturing business, and George Bancroft of Ponden remembered a Jonas Barraclough coming to his farm to repair a 'Barraclough' clock when he was 'nobbut a young 'un'.

Now Dollymoor is obliterated to make room for a different way of life, and along the valley above the reservoirs derelict farms stand, slowly decaying, and soon they, too, will be no more. In the past the Water Authority's policy has been to depopulate these farms because of possible sewage seepage (Ponden has been used for domestic purposes since 1971), but then a possible crack appeared in the system.

At ruined Lower Slack Farm above Ponden restoration work was done. The Water Authority granted a twenty-year lease to Bradford Metropolitan Council, and Lower Slack became an outdoor centre – most of the repair work being done under the Youth Opportunities Scheme. Reprieve for one moorland farm. But in 2003 the lease was up, the farm was sold and it became a private dwelling.

Another development at Ponden is the sailing club, whose colourful craft ruffle the serene waters of the reservoir and bring new life to the valley – some might say.

In prehistory, ice and water formed the valley, and water has shaped its unique character down the years – eventually destroying some things, such as the farms and the lifestyle they engendered, but creating and supporting other things such as the mills, the assured domestic water supply, even the sailing club. And still, on the moors and down the hills, the springs and little streams run and sparkle – contributing to the life and spirit of the valley as it is today.

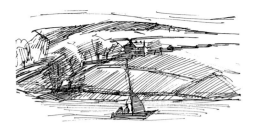

22

Ponden People

P onden Hall is that mystic blend of past and present, fact and fiction, that epitomises the Brontë moors. It stands on a promontory which used to be called 'The Scotchman's Arm' at the western end of Ponden Reservoir; at one side of the Hall the River Worth enters the reservoir, at the other side the Ponden Clough Beck.

For at least 350 years until 1898 it was the home of the Heaton family, although Heatons had connections with the Worth Valley as early as 1285, when William de Heton of Kirkheaton acquired Old Snap (or Owl Snape – snape meaning a tongue of land). The Heatons actually came to live at Old Snap in 1484 when John Heaton made it his home, and they gradually bought land at Ponden. The first Robert Heaton is recorded as owning land there, probably passed from his father, in 1560, and part of today's Ponden Hall could be his original house, considering for instance the timbered roof and Elizabethan fireplace of the East Gable bedroom.

The inscription carved over the entrance to the Hall is confusing: 'The Old House now standing was built by Robert Heaton for his son Michael Anno Domini 1634. The Old Porch and Peat House was built by his grandson Robert Heaton A.D. 1680. The present building was rebuilt by his descendant R.H. 1801.' The Robert mentioned first in the inscription is the son of the Robert who originally settled at Ponden, and most local scholars believe that the 'Old House' built for Michael and his bride is in fact the house which was until recently in ruins just below Ponden Hall, and that it was the original Elizabethan Hall which was extended in 1801, to give us the present building.

The Heatons prospered and spread initially over the Worth Valley, and then much further afield, and in each generation the names 'Robert' and 'Michael' alternated, thereby causing further confusion for historians. From being yeoman farmers they assumed the occupation of 'gentlemen' in the early seventeenth century, producing wool in vast quantities and keeping the cottages busy with woolcombing, spinning, scouring and weaving. They also owned stone quarries and a water-operated corn mill at Ponden, and in 1792, with cotton beginning to supplant the woollen industry, they built a cotton mill at Ponden, employing whole families including the children, and carts piled high with cotton twist rolled into Lancashire only two miles away.

Peacocks strolled in the garden of these 'gentlemen', vines provided raisin brandy as well as grapes for their bountiful table, and the bees in their wicker hives were taken to the moor in summer from the stone bee boles that can still be seen below the Hall, and supplied mead as well as honey.

Ponden Hall was a centre of culture in what has often been thought of as barren country, with a library containing thousands of books, some of which were rare and valuable; musical evenings were often held, and a brass band, augmented by local lads, practised and played in the small building behind the Hall which has recently been used as a bunkhouse for hikers on the Pennine Way. The house bulged with busyness and hospitality and the Heaton funeral 'biddings' were famous. This was an opportunity to gather all the kith and kin together, as well as friends and neighbours, and lists in existence today of all the 'bidden' guests show that even Ponden Hall must have been stretched to its limits on these occasions.

The Heatons were keen sportsmen and kept a pack of trencher-fed hounds, and one of their retainers, John Bolton of the mighty lungs, whose family had served at Ponden Hall for generations, was a famous huntsman. It was said that when John blew his horn at Ponden it could be heard as far away as Haworth Brow, and on his gravestone in Haworth churchyard are inscribed the words, 'Here lieth the Body of John Bolton . . . late Huntsman of Ponden . . .'.

Public responsibilities were also taken seriously by the Heatons. Andrew Heaton, who lived at Old Snap, was one of the first trustees of Haworth Church lands in 1559, a trusteeship held by generations of the Ponden Heatons until 1898. They were also churchwardens at Haworth, constables, grand jurymen and very much involved in tiny Scar Top Chapel. A lovely avenue of plane trees led from Ponden Hall to the chapel until Ponden Reservoir was built in 1876 and avenue and trees disappeared under the water. One responsibility they did shirk. Robert Heaton the third was offered a knighthood at the coronation of Charles I. For some reason he refused the honour and had to pay a composition of £10, the receipt for this £10 being signed by one Wentworth, King's Commissioner, who was later created Earl of Strafford – and later still beheaded. Perhaps Robert was wiser than he knew.

Ponden Hall, being the place it is, must have its ghost, and there is a story of a grey-bearded man, carrying a 'lanthorn', who appears from time to time from a westerly direction and enters the old walled garden. His visits were said to coincide with the imminent demise of a member of the Heaton family. At one time there was an attempt made to have him exorcised, but he was a persistent sort of ghost, his positively last appearance being made much later just before the deaths of the last two Heatons to live at Ponden Hall in 1898.

The Heatons and the Brontës were friends, and Emily in particular often used the Heaton library. Traditionally, Ponden Hall is the Thrushcross Grange of *Wuthering Heights*, and an incident in the Heaton family history could also have triggered Emily's imagination. Michael Heaton was killed during the civil wars and, strange for a man of property, left no will. His widow Anne, left with two small children, subsequently married a Henry Casson, of unknown origin, who proceeded to take over affairs at Ponden Hall and was actually called upon, as a man of substance, to

Moonrise over Ponden Reservoir.

swear an oath of allegiance to the Commonwealth. Anne and Henry had a son, John, and things looked black for Michael's heir, Robert, whose education had been so neglected that he could not sign his name on a legal document when he came of age in 1663. After nearly twenty years Anne finally managed to regain administration of the estate, but young Robert had to buy back his own household goods from Henry Casson for £13. Henry eventually faded back into oblivion, John Casson died unmarried in 1710 – and the Heaton inheritance was secure. So much for Heathcliff.

Another Heaton connection with *Wuthering Heights* could be the enormous Tudor carved oak cupboard which was a family possession for generations and which now stands in East Riddlesden Hall, Keighley, the property of the National Trust. Emily would no doubt see this cupboard when she visited the Heatons and describes a similar 'vast oak dresser' in the 'house' at 'Wuthering Heights'.

During the last part of Patrick Brontë's incumbency at Haworth, Ponden Hall was occupied by the 'five brethren', last in the long line of Ponden Heatons – Robert, William, John, Thomas Midgley and Michael. Although Robert, the eldest, was nominal head of the family, they all apparently lived in perfect harmony, even when John married and brought his wife to live at the Hall. Michael, the youngest, also married but went to live in Stanbury.

Their life was a little more 'low-key' than their illustrious ancestors, although they still continued to play a big part in the life of the neighbourhood and were always regarded as 'gentry'. Robert was a trustee of Haworth Church lands and served on many local committees, Thomas taught at Scar Top Chapel evening classes and took a great interest in young people and education generally, and John was a musician and was connected with the choir and music of Scar Top Chapel for forty-five years. He composed anthems and hymn tunes and one of these was sung at his funeral.

Robert and Thomas, the last of the 'brethren', died within eleven days of each other in 1898, just after the alleged last appearance of the Ponden ghost, and the property and its contents were put up for auction.

According to a contemporary newspaper report, the Oldfield schoolmaster was checking over the proofs of the catalogue of books in the library before the sale when he noticed some loose sheets lying about, printed in Elizabethan script. Closer inspection showed them to be a first folio edition of all Shakespeare's plays but one, dated 1623, and their presence at Ponden Hall would be quite feasible as the Heatons made business trips to London in the 1600s. The schoolmaster mentioned that the folio was not in the catalogue, but it never was included, and the entire collection of books, some of them very rare, realised about £75 at the sale, presumably under the hammer of a very incompetent auctioneer. At least one bargain must have gone for a song that day!

Ponden Hall was once again connected with weaving when Roderick and Brenda Taylor, trading as 'Brontë Tapestries', handloom weavers, moved there from Thornton. When I visited them in the 1970s the weaving studio was like an Aladdin's cave, a place where time had stood still. The walls of the studio were lined

Ponden Hall, where fact and fiction, past and present, come together. It was well known to the Brontë family, and many people think that Emily based her 'Thrushcross Grange' of Wuthering Heights *on this house. An old mounting block is in the foreground.*

with cones of wool in deep rich colours, glowing as flames leapt from an open fire in a Georgian hob grate and sent flickers on to an old beamed ceiling. Bales of lovely woven cloth were everywhere, rugs and mohair stoles were piled on a table, and a rail of handwoven tunics and jackets provided quite a temptation. Some students were having a weaving lesson on traditional counter-balanced floor handlooms, and one of them, looking at the colour all around her, said she felt 'like a kid with a paintbox'.

Then, unfortunately, mainly for economic reasons, the weaving was relegated to just a hobby, although the Taylors carried on the Ponden tradition of hospitality, but on a commercial basis. Ponden Hall lies on the Pennine Way, and provided a welcoming oasis for weary walkers, either in the bunkhouse or in the Hall itself, and of course other guests were welcome, too. Life at the Hall (the Taylors preferred to call it the 'Farm') was down-to-earth, and the kettle was always boiling on the hob.

At about that time an article appeared about Ponden Hall in a Japanese magazine, and Rod and Brenda were invaded by Japanese guests, many of them waving a copy of the article. 'We never did find out what it said because the Japanese could never translate it for us, but they always seemed to be having a good laugh, which made us wonder,' said Brenda.

It was not just the Japanese and the walkers who zoomed in on Ponden Hall. 'We get dozens of Heatons from all over the world, saying they are Ponden Heatons or they are related. One, from New Zealand, a Robert Heaton, vaguely knew that his family came from somewhere in the Keighley area. They found Ponden Hall after a visit to the Haworth Tourist Information Centre and told us they have a farm in New Zealand called Ponden Farm.'

Now Brenda has moved from Ponden Hall and has rebuilt Ponden House, opposite. She runs her 'hospitality business' from there, so a haven for walkers remains at Ponden. The Hall itself has become a private residence.

The Heatons have multiplied 'like the sand which is upon the sea-shore', and every one of them is proud of being a Heaton. A couple came all the way from sunny California to gaze on Ponden Hall, their ancestral home, and to meet with other Heatons in the area. They were old and frail but very determined, and the trip was their Golden Wedding celebration, the high point of their lives.

So, Ponden Hall still retains its fascination, and its past is like a magnet, drawing people to it in the present.

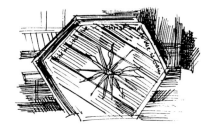

23

Methodism in his Madness

They called him 'Mad Grimshaw', but then people are often called mad who have positive ideas and the courage of their convictions. In fact, William Grimshaw was not always 'afflicted' that way.

He was born in Brindle, near Preston, in 1708 and entered Christ's College, Cambridge, as a 'sizar', or poor student, in 1726, where after a promising start he 'conformed' like the rest and succumbed to the fleshpots and, in his own words, 'falling in with bad company, learned to drink, swear and what not'!

When he left Cambridge he became a typical Church of England minister of the day – comfortable (although with a tendency to practical joking), fond of fishing, card playing, hunting and drinking, and totally inadequate in any spiritual crisis. He also married a dashing young widow called Sarah Sutcliffe, formerly Lockwood, who also happened to be an heiress. Her two brothers both died during childhood, the eldest, John, in 1710, the year she was born, and the youngest, William, in 1716, when he accidentally fell into a vat of 'liquor' during the annual family brew-up.

Grimshaw first became aware that his ministry was without substance shortly before his marriage in 1735, and then began the long haul that finally led to his full commitment to his God. At one point he even blamed his happy marriage for his spiritual struggles (which could account for his remarks many years later in Haworth that marriage was a snare for immature Christians). Even so, his wife's death in 1739 plunged him into a terrible slough of despond. He had kept a written record of his progress and eventually, like another Pilgrim, came to a 'place somewhat ascending' and lost his burden of torment. At about the same time two others had earned themselves the label of 'mad enthusiasts' for their evangelical zeal – their names were John and Charles Wesley.

Methodism was brought to Yorkshire by John Nelson, a stonemason from Birstall. He was working in London in 1739 when he heard John Wesley preaching and experienced a tremendous spiritual enlightenment. When he returned to Birstall soon afterwards, his own preaching was heard by a shoemaker from Keighley who invited him to preach in that town. The shoemaker, John Wilkinson, an unlettered man, subsequently became the first Methodist preacher in that area, and his extempore preaching so amazed a young draper called Colbeck that not only did he become the second Methodist preacher in Keighley but he also formed the first Wesleyan Society in Haworth in about 1744.

William Grimshaw came to Haworth in 1742, two years earlier, and had already started his own revival at the parish church, where it was eventually necessary to enlarge the building. His methods were unorthodox, probably a reaction to the general flabbiness of the Church at that time, and much has been said of his use of the horsewhip, of how he would set his congregation a long psalm and then leave them while he visited nearby hostelries to 'persuade' recalcitrants back to church. Once it is said he sent the churchwardens instead, and when they didn't return he went himself and found them drinking a pint of ale themselves. Great was the shindy in Haworth Church that morning.

Not as much has been said of how the people eventually flocked in their thousands to hear him preach, of their own accord, flooding out into the churchyard when the church itself was full. Grimshaw was a man of his times and times were rough, particularly in Haworth.

Living conditions were bad, few houses had their own water, sanitation was non-existent, and the main water pump stood next to a public cesspit and was supplied with water that ran through the churchyard. Sowdens, Grimshaw's house, had its own water pump, but in other respects, forgoing all refinement, he lived as basically as his parishioners in order to identify with them. His home was open house, and he often gave up his own bed for visitors, going to sleep in the loft. Sometimes he was found cleaning their shoes in the early morning before he thought anyone else was awake, and once 150 people crammed into his small rooms for a meeting.

The Revd William Grimshaw, sometimes called 'Mad Grimshaw', Haworth incumbent and stalwart supporter of John and Charles Wesley.

For all this saintliness Grimshaw was a full-blooded man, not given to half-measures. His constant railing against sensual pleasures earned him the name of 'puritan', but his past personal experience had shown him the grip they could have on a man. In 1743 Haworth Church went on record in the York Diocese as having the largest percentage of white-sheeted, bare-footed penitents doing public penance. This was not because Haworth was most wicked, but because its parson was most vigilant, and felt that this way his flock and his Master could best be served. He was so concerned for their eternal souls that he harangued the dying to repentance until their beds trembled beneath them – then tenderly cared for their physical needs.

Grimshaw himself was completely sincere, and had no time for spiritual hypocrisy in others. One of his flock set himself up to be extremely charitable, but Grimshaw had his doubts. He therefore dressed himself as a beggar and presented himself before this man, asking for a night's lodging. The response he got was anything but charitable, and one can imagine the tirade that followed.

Grimshaw and the people of Haworth understood each other, and he was greatly loved and respected by them; often he would walk miles across the moors, in any weather, at any time of day or night, to visit someone in need. His preaching also took him far and wide, and again he usually walked, often taking his own meal with him so as not to impose on anyone else. He was described by John Newton, one of his biographers who actually knew him, as 'a son of thunder, but also a son of consolation'. Can it be coincidence that the Greek for 'thunder' is 'bronte'?

He was also a man of great faith. Each year, at Haworth Tide, there was an event which grieved him deeply; horse-racing took place on Haworth Moor, illegally because of the lack of proper permits, and it attracted all the riff-raff of the area, being a 'scene of the grossest and most vulgar riots, profligacy and confusion'. Grimshaw had done all he could to have these races done away with, suggesting possible alternative attractions, but the people of Haworth stood firm – they would have their horse-racing. Eventually Grimshaw fell on his knees before God and left the matter in His hands. Just before the races were due to start it began to rain, and soon there was an absolute deluge which lasted for the three days the races were to be run. They had to be cancelled and from that year Haworth Tide was without its races.

The high wooden pews of the Haworth Church in those days were a temptation to doze or dissemble, but from his lofty triple-decker pulpit, with its sounding-board decorated with a blazing sun, Grimshaw could see all, and offenders were publicly reprimanded. Even the dogs that were brought to church by their owners had to behave themselves. Many churches had dog-whippers for quelling a disturbance during worship, but Grimshaw dealt with the problem himself, using his boot. Once during a service a dogfight got out of hand, and he yelled at those trying to deal with it, 'What, have you no feet!'

When Nelson came to preach Methodist doctrines in Haworth, Grimshaw at first would have nothing to do with it, forbidding his congregation to go and listen, but then came Will Darney, a Scottish shoemaker and pedlar, preaching as he peddled, and proud Grimshaw became his assistant. In May 1747 John Wesley made the first of many visits to Haworth and a great bond was formed between him and William Grimshaw. Haworth became a base for Methodist preachers who travelled miles through Lancashire and Yorkshire, the area around Haworth being known as 'Grimshaw's Round'. This gut-religion appealed very much to the people of the moors. At first Methodism was confined to the Established Church and many hoped it would stay within those bounds, but in the following century it finally broke away – the Methodist Church had become a separate entity.

It has been said that the Methodist Revival saved England from a social revolution very similar to that experienced by France, coinciding as it did with the upheaval caused by our Industrial Revolution. Maybe so. Certainly country communities and ways of life had been changed, and the old paternalistic system gradually disappeared as mechanised industry swept the land.

At the same time, in the valleys of the West Riding, chapels sprang up like mushrooms in the night, some with pretensions to Doric styling, others definitely 'barnic'. The chapels flourished, supported by local manufacturers, who in turn were supported by their workforce, and they provided general educational classes as well as religious instruction. These classes were a feature of village life, and Whit Walks were a highlight of the year, sometimes with brass bands preceding the walkers and teas being provided in the gardens of the gentry. The churches also had their walks and there are stories told in Oakworth of processions from rival denominations setting off from different ends of the village and meeting somewhere in the middle. The footpath was narrow and so was the road, and one of the excitements of the 'Walk' was deciding who was going to give way to whom when the confrontation occurred. The 'Charities' or Anniversaries were carefully planned so as not to clash with anybody else's, and great was the rivalry thereat – Sundays through the summer were taken up with visiting on these special occasions. People felt the security of 'belonging' to a close-knit community provided by the chapels.

Grimshaw was the instigator when a Methodist Chapel was built on West Lane, Haworth, in 1758, and became one of the trustees, along with the Wesleys and Thomas Colbeck. Carved above a window of the chapel is Grimshaw's favourite text: 'To us to live is Christ, to die is gain.' (This text also appears, painted in letters of gold, on Aunt Branwell's teapot in the Parsonage Museum, strangely moving when you consider her sacrificial life.)

Today the cause of Methodism has altered in the valley. Some chapels have disappeared altogether, others have been converted into self-conscious country cottages, and one in Keighley, famous for its renderings of the *Messiah* in days gone by, is now a mosque. A few Charities still take place, but one feels that the tide is running out. No doubt Grimshaw's methods would be unacceptable in most chapels and churches today. He would be considered an eccentric and an embarrassment. But when you come to think of it, most reformers are an embarrassment to somebody.

24

The Company of Ghosts

To walk up Haworth Main Street on a grey winter's day is to be followed by a company of ghosts. On each side the houses close in, unyielding millstone grit, leaning towards each other in the mist, and the only sound is of water dripping off the roofs, remorseless as the passing of time but making no impression on the stone beneath. Haworth on a day like this becomes a place out of time, a backdrop for happenings and people long since gone. Even the double yellow lines on each side of the stone setts (Haworth Main Street is not cobbled), put there by an insensitive Bradford Metropolitan Council, fade as the company passes and the mist parts, dissolves up the alleys and re-forms.

Past members of Haworth band lead the company, all local lads, returning in the early hours triumphant from a band contest, playing lustily but – or so the story goes – walking softly in stockinged feet in deference to the sleeping villagers.

Behind the band comes a solitary figure wearing a Father Christmas outfit – George Greaves, who for many years paid his own particular tribute at the Christmas Eve Communion Service. He chose his time well, and at the quietest part of the service, when the congregation was kneeling, he would appear at the back of the church in a bedraggled Father Christmas outfit, complete with jingling bells, and walk slowly down the centre aisle to the chancel. There he solemnly bowed to the altar before making the same dignified progress back up the church. The congregation was breathless, the Rector white-faced in the Christmas tree glow, wondering what George was going to do next, but his performance never varied – he simply made his contribution to the Christmas celebration, then vanished into the night.

Next in the company walks Jim Luty, wearing his Sunday-best outfit of white cord trousers, velvet jacket, coloured waistcoat and straw 'benji'. Locally known as 'Charlie Rock', he was a mill worker who hawked sticks of aniseed and peppermint rock in his spare time, mostly to the patrons of the local hostelries.

Once he was emerging from the King's Arms when a Salvation Army lassie approached him with a collection box. He felt shamed into putting a mean penny-piece into the box, then bolted into the pub for another drink, where he discovered to his horror that he'd donated a half-crown instead of a penny. Now Charlie was a man of action and set off down Main Street like a pint from a pump, racing along

Haworth Main Street at dusk.

Sun Street to where the Salvation Army Citadel stood by the old ducking-stool well. A service was just starting and the Captain, seeing Charlie enter and mistaking him for a penitent sinner, invited him to the front. Charlie went forward, explained his dilemma – and asked for his half-crown back.

'Would you take back money that's already been blessed in the service of the Lord?' asked the Captain. 'Aye lad. If Ah doan't Ah shall be buggered next week,' was Charlie's reply.

Following Charlie Rock comes 'Old Tooit', the village barber, patronised by Patrick Brontë. Renowned for his practical jokes, he is reputed to have shaved just half of a customer's face to pay off a score, and to have gained admission to hospital out of visiting times to see a friend by turning his collar back to front and posing as a parson. His real name: Jack Toothill; his tariff: two shaves a week for 1½*d* the job lot, single shaves 1*d*, haircuts 1½*d* a time. His wooden shop was transferred complete from Bridgehouse Lane to Butt Lane on a hay sleigh and had the distinction of being the first shop in Haworth to be lit by electricity – but only when the annual fair came to the field below, where the park now stands. 'Old Tooit' simply plugged in to their electricity generators.

'Old Hake' comes next. He was a drover who settled in Haworth as odd-job man and slept rough mostly. His real name was John Pickles and in his faded raincoat, hobnailed boots and battered trilby he could usually be found sitting in an old chair by the church steps, accepting drinks from anybody who would buy him one, and heckling the temperance meetings that were held there.

And so the company passes – a host of characters shaped by the spirit that is Haworth and who have, in their turn, left something of themselves there.

'Joe Pop', Joseph Crabtree, one-time owner of a grocer's and off-licence shop in Main Street that sold everything from jam to zinc baths, and who graced the local fêtes and galas in a fine governess cart . . . Willie Hardiman, who lived alone on Sun Street and habitually wore an old bowler, baggy trousers and gaping shoes. He regularly covered most of Haworth on foot to deliver free copies of the *Haworth Advertiser*. Generously bearded, lame and with a deformed hand, he sold matches as a sideline. He was not over-fastidious about washing and was an object of curiosity and even fear to the local children, who congregated outside his house to gape at him.

Sam Bancroft, butcher and gamekeeper, who was a garrulous man, known to have been at a loss for words only once in his life – when he appeared on Wilfred Pickles' *Have a Go* on BBC Radio. He was regularly seen scanning the moors with his telescope. Why? Nobody seems to know. Perhaps it was a throw-back to his *Dad's Army* days when he patrolled them against possible invasion. Foster Bannister, Captain of the local Fire Brigade when Haworth didn't have an engine, only a hand pump, and who also doubled up as trombone player in the band. Jim Knowles, a quarryman renowned for his economies, welcomed evening visitors to his home by candlelight. Once seated, and with conversation flowing, he would blow out the candle. 'We can talk in't dark as well as in't leet,' was his philosophy.

Seven covered wagons, with wooden wheels that make no sound as they labour up the steep street, bring up the rear of the company, having travelled a day's journey from Thornton, nine miles away. They contain the entire possessions of the family that is to make Haworth world-famous and encapsulate the district in their writings – although even these writings cannot compare with their own poignant story. A much-maligned Victorian father, a delicate mother and six young children peer anxiously through the mist at the place that is to be their home for the rest of their lives.

Hovering in the background is the figure of Willie Weightman, 'Celia Amelia', the talented and fun-loving curate who walked all the way to Bradford to buy and post a Valentine card for the Brontë girls when he heard that they'd never received one – or so the story goes.

At last the company is gone, and Haworth Main Street is empty once more. Can they ever be replaced, these singular people, or do modern times make stereotypes of us all and carbon copies of our towns and villages?

'Haworth is just a shell – it's an empty place,' was Jack Laycock's heartfelt comment when I talked to him just before he died. Jack had lived in Haworth since he was four and was a familiar figure in and around the parish church where he was warden.

He looked back with nostalgia to the time when Haworth was a self-contained village, with life revolving round its numerous chapels and church. It boasted two cinemas, four tennis clubs, three cricket clubs and three football clubs and its own private bus company. Regular services on the Worth Valley Railway made possible a trip to Morecambe for half-a-crown and a night out dancing at the Winter Gardens, just for a change from the local weekly dances.

Haworth Band was the village band in those days, the appointment of its conductor was a village issue and the band featured at every village function. Overall pay was £10 plus tea, £12 without it. On summer Sunday afternoons and evenings, they gave concerts in the schoolyard on their portable bandstand, transferring to Haworth Park when it was made, and toured the area on Christmas Day to play at the homes of 'the gentry'. Now it seems that less than half the musicians are Haworth residents and their fees are generally considered too high for local engagements.

'We were poor in those days – if you had a front room you were middle class, everybody had outside toilets and most had matting on the floor during the week. It was taken up on Saturday night and a carpet put down for Sunday, which was a day of rest. Everybody dressed smartly on a Sunday – caps and bowlers were the fashion. We had a new suit every year for Easter, even if it was only a cheap one, and we saved up for it, so much a week at the Co-op. Your year was planned out for you in the village, even the children had whip-and-top time and hoop-and-stick time, and the same things happened at the same time each year – it had a stabilising influence.'

Jack blamed the 'death' of the Haworth he knew on many things – television, a decline of chapel and church life, children attending different schools and not getting to know each other, the motor car – and that remote ogre, Bradford

Metropolitan Council. 'Haworth Urban District Council just about planned, built and upheld Haworth – we had our own gas, electricity, sewage and waterworks. Then we went under Keighley and managed to fit in, but being under Bradford is ruining village life.'

At the present time Haworth has a lot of 'off-comed 'uns' (they do say you're an 'off-comed 'un' in Haworth until you've lived there for forty years), many of them living in new housing estates and commuting to Leeds, Bradford or Keighley, and they bring new ideas which are not always acceptable to the older residents. Cars enable people to find more sophisticated entertainment than Haworth occasionally provides, and both its cinemas are closed. There are still some long-established family shops – but many prefer to patronise the supermarkets and shops of nearby towns.

Most of the textile mills, formerly Haworth's life-blood, have either disappeared altogether or gone over to the production of other things.

Each year thousands of tourists descend upon Haworth, attracted by the railway or the Brontës, and no doubt they find what they have come looking for, be it the souvenir shops, cafés, the museum and church, or the moors. They are a source of frustration to some residents, income to others who do 'bed and breakfast', business to the shops and satisfaction to the Brontë Parsonage Museum.

In spite of all this – the tourists and the inevitable wrangles – or perhaps even because of it, Haworth today still maintains a strong, determined character. It has a unique essence, and a charm that is indefinable – and it is still possible to walk up its Main Street and be followed by a company of ghosts.